MAKING ENDS MEET $

Henry Edward Felder

Making Ends Meet

Financial Planning for the Christian Family

REVIEW AND HERALD® PUBLISHING ASSOCIATION
HAGERSTOWN, MD 21740

The author assumes full responsibility for the accuracy of all facts and quotations as cited in this book.

This book was
Edited by Richard W. Coffen
Designed by Patricia S. Wegh
Cover design by Helcio Deslandes
Typeset: 11/13.5 Times

PRINTED IN U.S.A.

99 98 97 96 95 94 5 4 3 2 1

R&H Cataloging Service
Felder, Henry Edward, 1943-
Making ends meet.

1. Personal finance. I. Title.
332.024

ISBN 0-8280-0789-6

With Dedication

To my dear
and loving wife, Clara,
whose constant inspiration
made this book possible.

Contents

1

INTRODUCTION

THE CHRISTIAN FAMILY living in the United States and on the threshold of the twenty-first century faces financial problems and issues that were not part of the early experiences of first-century Christians or even of Christians of the past century. On any given day, the family makes dozens of decisions that have consequences for its financial well-being.

Do Christians Need Financial Planning?

The Christian family finds itself having to make many decisions involving money—such as where to live, whether or not to buy a car, or how best to finance Christian education. Virtually all these financial decisions involve money to be used in the present or the future. Consequently, these decisions require some form of strategy—financial planning.

In Matthew 6:25 Jesus says, "Take no thought for your life, what ye shall eat, or what ye shall drink." So should the Christian family engage in financial planning? For many Christian families this question poses a real dilemma. However, we need to realize that in the complex society in which we live, financial planning will take place either through conscious effort or by default.

If financial planning is by design, the decision-making can be so structured that we seek God's will as we handle the resources He has entrusted to us. When properly done, financial planning makes us akin to the wise man who invested his money and was able to return to his lord a doubling of the funds entrusted to him (Matt. 25:21).

However, one might ask, Since we expect the soon return of our Lord, isn't financial planning a waste of time? First, we must remember that we do not know the day or the hour when our Lord shall return. "But of that day and hour knoweth no man" (Matt. 24:36). Second, a popular misconception is that financial planning involves only events in the *distant* future. True financial planning includes decisions that will have an impact on the present, as well as on the future—immediate and distant.

Therefore, living in the present requires financial planning of some type. Financial planning involves practical, everyday types of events, as well as future events, such as retirement. Financial planning, rather than indicating a lack of faith, is a way to bring greater harmony and order into an activity that is vital to the life of every Christian's—prudent management of God's resources.

What Is Christian Financial Planning?

Christian financial planning is distinguished from ordinary financial planning by several characteristics:

- Christian financial planning puts Christ at the center of all activities and seeks His presence in all goals and courses of action.
- Christian financial planning recognizes divine ownership of all resources, but it also recognizes human stewardship of those resources.
- Christian financial planning takes into consideration that this world is but a way station along the route to something infinitely greater and better.

Christ is all in all.—"Christ is all, and in all" (Col. 3:11). So the Christian's first commitment is to Jesus Christ. To Him—and Him alone—does the Christian owe allegiance and reverence. Paul says, "For to me to live is Christ." (Phil. 1:21). When we focus on the cross of Christ, everything else falls into proper perspective. Because we are bought with a price, our highest duty is to serve Him. This includes our financial planning.

FINANCIAL PLANNING IS AN ACTIVITY THAT REQUIRES ESTABLISHING A SYSTEMATIC COURSE OF ACTION REGARDING FINANCIAL MATTERS, BEGINNING WITH A STATEMENT OF GOALS.*

Perhaps one of the finest expressions of Christ's role in the financial life of the Christian is found in Jesus' famous sermon on the mount. Jesus said, "But seek ye first the kingdom of God, and his righteousness; and all these things shall be added unto you" (Matt. 6:33). This is not a promise of wealth, health, or happiness. It is a promise of God's presence. And it is His presence that governs Christian financial planning.

Christians are stewards of God's possessions.—David said of the Lord, "For all things come of thee, and of thine own have we given thee" (1 Chron. 29:14). Truly, all good things come from a loving heavenly Father. Life. Health. Strength. The ability to gain wealth.

One Christian writer has put it this way: "We belong to God; we are His sons and daughters—His by creation, and His by the gift of His only-begotten Son for our redemption. . . . The mind, the heart, the will, and the affections belong to God; the money that we handle is the Lord's. Every good that we receive and enjoy is the result of divine benevolence. God is the bountiful giver of all good, and He desires that there shall be an acknowledgment, on the part of the receiver, of these gifts that provide for every necessity of the body and the soul" (Ellen G. White, *Counsels on Stewardship*, p. 72).

"Moreover it is required in stewards, that a man be found faithful" (1 Cor. 4:2). This faithfulness manifests itself in the return of tithes and offerings to the Lord (Mal. 3:8-10), because the tithe is holy unto the Lord (Lev. 27:30).

This world is not where the Christian's real treasure is.—Jesus said, "Do not store up for yourselves treasures on earth. . . . But store up for yourselves treasures in heaven. . . . For where your treasure is, there your heart will be also" (Matt. 6:19-21, NIV).

This principle means that the Christian's focus is not this world—although financial planning is very much a part of this world. Christians know that hoarding, coveting, accumulation for the sake of accumulation, and the love of money are *not* what financial planning should be about. So while prudent Christians lay up treasure in heaven, they also plan carefully for life in this world.

Use of This Book

Several things are to be stressed in the use of this book:

- This book is intended only as a window into financial planning and money management for the Christian family. The family is encouraged to read supplemental material and seek professional help when that seems appropriate.
- Throughout this book there is a heavy emphasis on the use of numbers, tables, and charts. These are there to help you understand just

where you stand financially.

- The illustrations in this book are true-to-life descriptions of the world of financial planning. However, they should not be used as absolute indicators.
- The financial world is constantly changing. Some indicators, such as interest rates, may vary considerably from what is presented here.

This book is structured by major topic for ease of reading. The next chapter provides details of the economic world in which we live. It discusses the concept of the *fundamental relationship* of finance. This is followed by chapters on the basic topics of income, savings, spending, and borrowing. Following these topics, there are discussions of such things as risk management, life insurance, retirement, and estate planning.

---

*Jerry M. Rosenberg, *Dictionary of Business and Management*, (New York: Wiley and Sons, 1983), p. 381.

2

How the Financial Fundamentals Work

Should the Christian family buy a house or rent one? Should the slightly old (but still usable) car be traded in for a more reliable (but much more expensive) new car? And what about debt? life insurance? savings?

Every year the average family makes thousands of economic decisions, some of which are trivial and involve nothing more complicated than deciding whether or not to eat at a restaurant or at home. Many other decisions, however, may involve such long-term obligations as estate planning, home purchases, or family additions.

Money Is the Central Thread in Financial Planning

The central thread throughout is money. By itself, money is neutral—neither good nor bad. However, inordinate affection devoted to its acquisition can destroy spirituality. How do Christians plan the wise use of their money? Some Christians may feel that the very act of planning may exhibit a lack of faith. Did not Christ Himself say, "Therefore I tell you, do not worry about your life, what you will eat or drink; or about your body, what you will wear. Is not life more important than food, and the body more important than clothes?" (Matt. 6:25)?

Christians need not worry themselves sick. But in this modern society an absence of planned use of the resources with which we have been entrusted may lead to Christians robbing God as well as themselves. The Bible explicitly requires good stewardship. The implication of 1 Timothy 5:8 is clear: "But if any provide not for his own, and specially for those of his own house, he hath denied the faith, and is worse than an infidel" (KJV). Christians who do not plan for the financial needs of family are worse than unbelievers!

Financial planning, like planning for anything else, involves a systematic approach to a problem. In this instance, the problem is that of money management. Through wise financial planning, the Christian family may make exceedingly better use of its resources and have the ability to return to God far fairer tithes and offerings. Indeed, the whole family can be made better off.

Before we begin a systematic study of financial planning, it is helpful to understand some basic rules and myths regarding it. These rules may be used in setting up a philosophy for guiding the family's approach to financial planning. The myths, of course, are things to be careful about.

The Rules of Christian Financial Planning

Rule 1—Apart from a few basic principles regarding avarice and greed, the Bible does not establish theologically correct ways to conduct financial planning.

Rule 2—Each family must establish for itself that pattern of financial planning that best meets its needs. There are no fixed formulas for all families.

These rules tell us that much of financial planning is *cultural*. The basic biblical injunction is about preferring money over service to God and humanity. The rules also say that each family must adopt a style in its financial planning that it can feel comfortable with. This can be done through prayerful, thoughtful discussion between members of the family. Where necessary, a financial consultant or counselor may assist. In addition, libraries have numerous books that can provide valuable information.

Myths of Christian Financial Planning

Financial planning is often encumbered by several slow-to-die myths.

Myth 1—"Money is the root of all evil." It is not money but the *love* of money that is the root of all evil (1 Tim. 6:10).

Myth 2—Only spiritually deficient persons will spend more than just passing moments on financial management. Much of the quality of life depends on the prudent use of the resources God has entrusted to us. This will frequently require prayerful, thoughtful planning.

Myth 3—What works for one Christian family under one set of circumstances must work for all families at all times.

Myth 4—Social custom and the prevailing environment do not affect the manner in which the family makes financial decisions.

These myths should *not* be a part of how the Christian family relates to financial planning.

Conditions That Affect Financial Planning

In addition to the impact of social custom and the prevailing environment, the following characteristics have a large impact on the Christian family's approach to financial planning:

- number of adults in the family
- family size and the ages of family members
- number of family members who work outside the home
- family beliefs about income sharing and pooling
- the short- and long-term goals of the family
- the family's basic set of values

Each of these dimensions is an integral part of the development of a consistent and systematic financial plan for the Christian family.

The Fundamental Relationship of Financial Planning

	The Major Components of Financial Planning	
Sources of Money	Income	Borrowing
Uses of Money	Spending	Saving

These components are related through what is called the "fundamental relationship of financial planning and management." All financial activity is either a *source of money* or a *use of money*. This relationship holds for all family financial arrangements and is defined as follows:

INCOME + BORROWING = SPENDING + SAVINGS

In short, family income plus family borrowing must equal family spending plus family savings. This relationship assumes, of course, that families do not destroy money and that giving money away is viewed in the same way as spending it.

This fundamental relationship does not take account of gifts, unless they are gifts of financial instruments such as money, stocks, or bonds. Thus, a gift vase of enormous worth will not be part of the fundamental relationship unless it is sold. Then the proceeds from the sale become income.

The *income component* includes all sources of income available to the family from wages, nonwage sources, government transfers, and gifts. The *borrowing component* involves all cash borrowing and all deferred payments for goods and services. This component includes loans and all debts.

The sum of all income and borrowing at a given interval of time sets a boundary for the amount of goods and services that the family can receive. *It is the family's "budget constraint."*

The ultimate objective of all income and borrowing is the spending and savings decisions made by the family. *Spending* may be for current consumption of goods and services, for gifts to individuals or organizations, or for future consumption through savings. Assets or income set aside as bequests to the church or to individuals are a form of present consumption. *Savings* are assets or income set aside for retirement or for a "rainy day." Savings are *future* consumption.

Using the fundamental relationship, we can begin to see how financial planning and asset management are useful tools for the Christian family. Once we come to understand this relationship, we can develop an approach to financial planning that encompasses the needs of any family.

The Economic Environment Affects Financial Planning

All financial planning is done in light of the existing economic environment. This environment includes inflation, interest payments, compounding, and discounting. For some families, unemployment means that income is restricted and that government transfer payments may have to be received. In this section the fundamental relationship is adjusted to account for the economic environment.

Time Affects Financial Planning

The fundamental relationship, and therefore the family's financial plan, is always time-related. As such, a financial plan is defined for a specific period of time and will be affected by the passage of time. Usually the time period will depend on the specific goals of the plan.

A *time horizon* is a planning period for an activity. The time horizon for a goal may be as short as a few months or as long as a lifetime. Those plans or goals that have a short time horizon will likely require different planning than goals with a long time horizon. For example, planning for a new car involves an entirely different set of activities from planning for the education of children.

The Christian family has an eternal time horizon. Ultimately all matters involve the Christian's eternal salvation, and that transcends any temporal time horizons or activities. But for the present, it is necessary to plan according to the time horizons that we place on activities. The time horizon means that we set goals, plan for the accomplishment of those goals, and seek to manage our resources in a way that accomplishes those goals.

The Christian family may set as goals any of the following activities:

- budgeting for educational and college expenses
- saving for a special church offering
- balancing a monthly budget
- saving to purchase a house or new car
- planning a family vacation
- accommodating an increase in the size of the family
- planning for retirement
- other appropriate goals

All goals involve time.—All goals involve time. Time to plan. Time to accumulate money in order to finance the goal. Time before the goals come to pass. Thus one part of a financial plan may involve a year, whereas another part may take five or more years to come to fruition. As time passes, the cost of achieving these goals changes—usually by making these goals more expensive. This change is what we call inflation.

INFLATION IS THE RATE AT WHICH PRICES OR INCOME CHANGES, EXPRESSED AS AN ANNUAL PERCENTAGE.

What Happens When Inflation Is High?

Inflation affects each financial goal or plan differently and must always be taken into account. In recent times inflation in the United States has increased at rates as low as 2 percent and as high as 10 percent. Inflation causes all items to cost more in nominal dollars over a period of time. Another way to look at inflation is how it erodes the purchasing power of money.

Figure 1 shows what future costs will be when goods that cost $100 in the base year are impacted by different rates of inflation for differing periods of time. After five years at 4 percent inflation (the rate in late 1992), those goods will cost $122. If the inflation rate is 8 percent (as it was in late 1979), those same goods will cost $147. After 15 years, the goods that cost $100 will cost $180 if the inflation rate is 4 percent, and a whopping $418 if the inflation rate goes up to 10 percent.

Figure 1
Impact of Inflation on $100

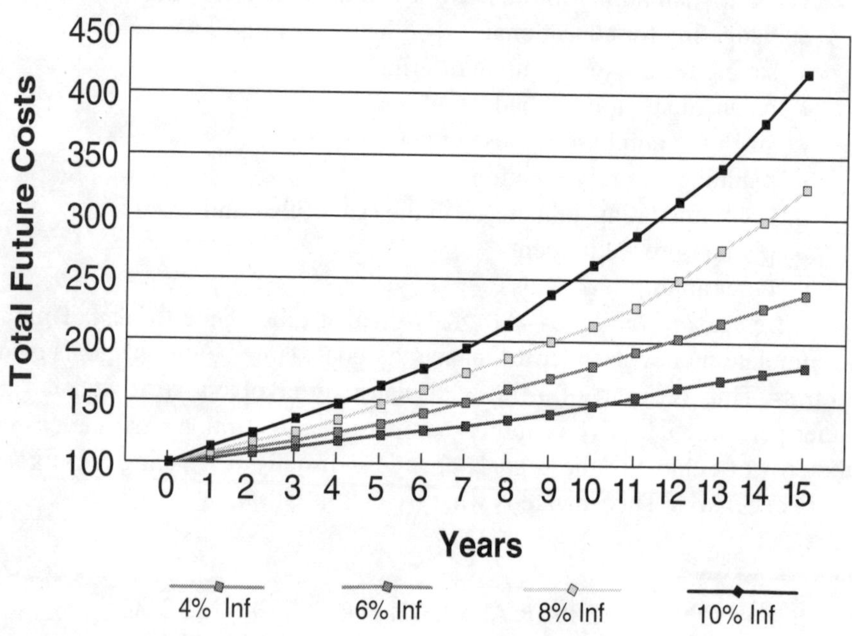

Figure 2 shows what happens to the purchasing power of income eroded by inflation. In this instance, look at what happens if you have $3,000 in monthly income. After five years of 4 percent inflation, you will have the purchasing power equal to only $2,446. After five years, at the inflation rate of 10 percent, your purchasing power is only $1,771.

Figure 2
Impact of Inflation on Purchasing Power

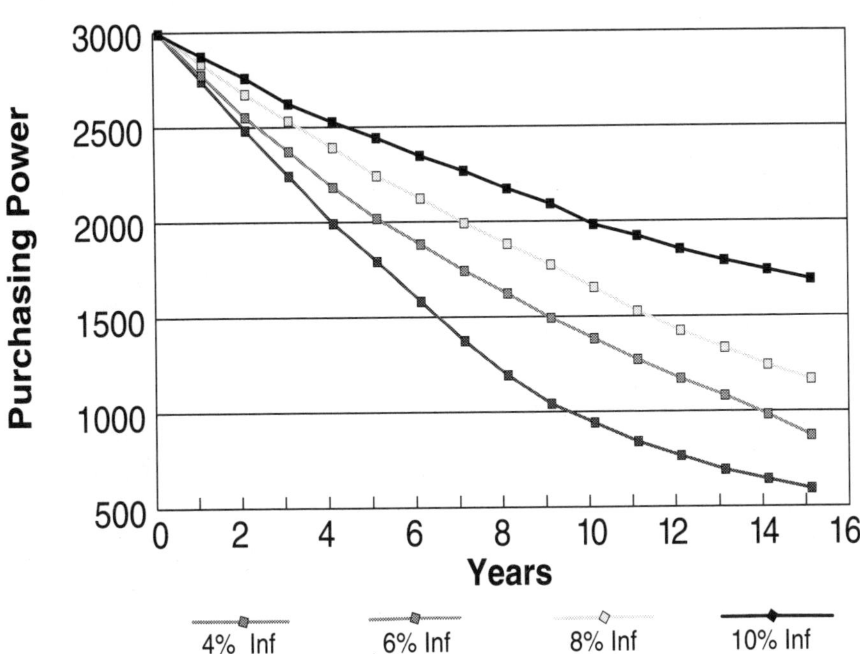

Since inflation affects the prices of everything, careful planning must go into all financial activities that involve time or the delay in purchases.

Inflation erodes the value of any fixed income. It also affects such things as church contributions. The acceptable $1.00 in church offering given 10 years ago will purchase the equivalent of only $.67 by 1993 (4 percent inflation).

Inflation is especially hard on people whose income remains fixed for long periods of time. For example, in planning for retirement the family must consider how the income needs will grow throughout the retirement period. A man or woman who retires at age 65 on a fixed income and who lives until the age of 75 could experience a purchasing power erosion as shown in Figure 2. As a result, the pension income may not be adequate to provide for the later years, unless it includes a cost-of-living adjustment factor (more on that later).

The CPI Is Used to Define Inflation

Every month the federal government publishes a series of statistics called the consumer price index (CPI). It is the official statement of the existing rate of inflation for a bundle of typical consumer purchases. The CPI is derived by examining the prices charged for a representative collection of consumer goods, including such items as food, clothing, medical care, and housing. The average cost for this bundle is then compared each month to show how prices have changed. Usually the CPI is shown as an annual rate.

There are other indicators of inflation, but the CPI is the most important. (Information about the CPI may be found in any standard almanac or in the financial sections of special business publications.)

The relationship between the rate of change in family *income* and the rate of change in *prices* as reflected in the CPI is summarized in Exhibit 1:

Exhibit 1

Income Increases Versus	Price Increases
IF	THEN
Income is rising faster than prices	The family is better off
Income is rising at the same rate as prices	The family remains the same
Income is rising at a slower rate than prices	The family is worse off

If family income is rising *faster* than the rate of inflation, the family will have increased purchasing power. From a financial perspective, the family is better off. Conversely, if family income is rising *more slowly* than prices, the family will have reduced purchasing power.

To reduce the negative effects of inflation, the family should: (1) monitor carefully the rate at which the income is growing relative to the annual CPI; (2) plan future spending and saving to account for inflationary effects; and (3) seek income increases that grow at a rate that is no less than the CPI.

The Role of Interest Rates

Interest rates play a very important role in two of the components of the fundamental relationship—borrowing and savings. When a family borrows (uses someone else's money) or delays paying for goods or services, it usually has to *pay* interest. When the family saves (lets someone else use its money), it *receives* interest payments.

INTEREST RATES ARE THE FEES PAID FOR THE USE OF SOMEONE ELSE'S MONEY.

The interaction of interest charges with *borrowing* and *saving* can be seen more clearly if we modify the fundamental relationship of financial management to include interest:

INCOME + BORROWING (MINUS INTEREST)
= SPENDING + SAVINGS (PLUS INTEREST)

The first term, *income + borrowing (**minus** interest),* represents the maximum limit on the family's ability to buy goods and savings. This is the family's budgetary constraint.

The second term, *spending + savings (**plus** interest),* represents the manner in which the family actually buys goods and services.

Through the process of borrowing, families are able to extend their control over more funds and goods than they would have been able to purchase otherwise. It permits the family to buy capital items of high prices. It allows the family to own homes and buy cars, furniture, appliances, and clothes that would otherwise have to be paid for in cash.

However, borrowing exacts the price of the interest charged on the money borrowed, and so it reduces the ability to consume in the future when the debt must be paid. (Later on we shall examine some of the insidious aspects of debt and explain why the Christian family should be very careful of the type and amount of debt it incurs.)

What determines the amount of interest charged?—Interest rates for borrowing vary so much because they reflect the ease with which the money is obtained, the collateral posted as surety for the loan, the lender's trust that the money will be repaid, and the individual's past history of credit behavior. The interest rate also varies with the condition of the economy. Table 1 shows the ranges of interest rates charged from various sources.

Table 1
Comparative Interest Rates

Borrowing		Savings	
Source	Annual Interest Rates	Source	Annual Interst Rates
Life Insurance Cash Value	3-6%	Life Insurance Policy	2-4%
Employee Credit Union	6-8%	Bank Christmas Club	3-5%
Credit Cards	9-21%	Bank Savings	3-6%
Bank Loans	8-12%	Savings and Loan Associations	3-7%
Savings and Loan Associations	10-16%	Certificates of Deposit	3-5%
Finance Companies	18-24%	Money Market Funds	3-5%
Pawn Shops	36-100%	Treasury Bonds	3-6%

NOTE: These rates are based on the 1993 "prime rate," the rate that banks charge their best customers. These figures are comparative; your rates may vary according to your credit rating and other factors.

From Table 1 we see that usually the least expensive way to borrow money is from the "cash surrender value" of a *life insurance policy*, with rates ranging from 3 to 6 percent. (Such borrowing reduces the face value of the life insurance by the amount borrowed.)

An employee *credit union* is another source of relatively low interest rates for borrowing. Depending on the reason for the loan, credit unions in 1992 charged as little as 6 to 8 percent for funds for cars, vacations, home improvements, and other uses.

The most expensive interest rates are those charged by *finance companies* and *pawn shops*. These rates can range from 18 percent for finance companies to as much as 100 percent for pawn shops. Individuals use these sources of loans when their credit history and income will not permit them to secure loans from more conventional sources.

It must be stressed that not all borrowing sources are desirable for use by all families. Only under the most desperate conditions would a family borrow money from the high-cost sources of funds.

The amount of *interest earned* on savings varies primarily by the institution in which funds are deposited. The interest paid on savings does not vary as much as the interest charged for borrowing. As is clear from Table 1, interest payments tend to be much less than interest charges.

Banks are a traditional place to deposit funds, and in 1992 they paid, on average, 3.5 percent interest on deposited funds. The lowest interest rates paid on savings are frequently those that come from the savings component of a life insurance policy. Since for many families such policies represent forced savings, the lower return is acceptable to them since they help the family accumulate assets. In addition, an insurance policy is part of this forced savings (more will be said about this later).

Probably the most frivolous type of savings account is the "Christmas Club" savings plan. Under this plan, the family sets aside a fixed amount each week and receives a lump-sum payment in time for Christmas purchases. However, the same bank generally pays a higher return on a simple savings account. The family is paying, in the form of lower interest income, for its lack of discipline in savings.

The power of compounding—Something amazing happens when money is set aside on a regular basis and the interest is allowed to accumulate. In addition to the interest being paid on the principal funds invested, interest is also paid on the previously paid interest! The result is that the funds grow at a much faster rate. This is the power of *compounding*.

There are two primary types of compounding of funds:

- investment of a single amount that is allowed to accumulate
- investment of a given amount periodically (each month or year, for example)

Figure 3 and Table 2 show what happens when a single investment of $1,000 is allowed to compound at varying rates during a period of time. After 20 years at 6 percent interest earned, the single investment is worth $3,207. However, if the interest rate is doubled to 12 percent, the single investment soars to $9,646—more than triple the value of the investment at 6 percent! This reflects the fact that you are getting interest on your interest. For each $1,000 payment you set aside at age 35 and allow to compound at 12 percent, you will have $29,960 at age 65!

Figure 3
Compound Value of Single $1,000 Payment

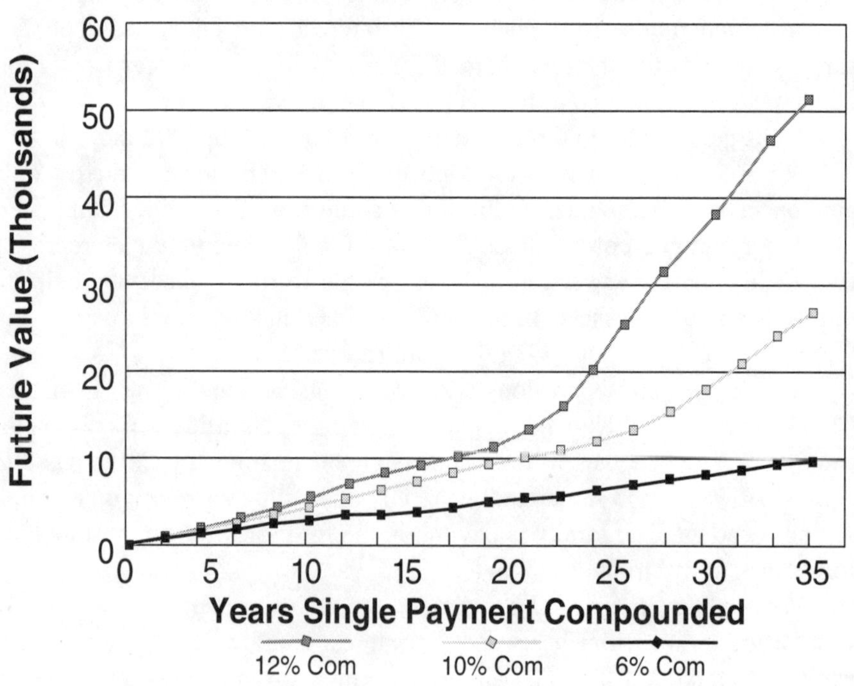

Table 2
Future Value of a Single $1,000 Investment

	Anual Rate of Return		
	6%	10%	12%
Year	Value at End of the Year		
1	$ 1,060	$ 1,100	$ 1,120
2	1,124	1,210	1,254
4	1,262	1,464	1,574
6	1,419	1,772	1,974
8	1,594	2,144	2,476
10	1,791	2,594	3,106
12	2,012	3,138	3,896
14	2,261	3,797	4,887
16	2,540	4,595	6,130
18	2,854	5,560	7,690
20	3,207	6,727	9,646
22	3,604	8,140	12,100
24	4,049	9,850	15,179
26	4,549	11,918	19,040
28	5,112	14,421	23,884
30	5,743	17,449	29,960
32	6,453	21,114	37,582
34	7,251	25,548	47,143
36	7,686	28,102	52,800

SOURCE: Calculations by author. Amounts compounded annually; assumes that all interest payments are reinvested.

The power of an annuity —An annuity is even more powerful than simple compounding, but it requires two things: (1) setting aside a fixed amount each period and (2) maintaining a constant rate of return on the amount set aside. Look at what happens when you invest as little as $100 per month at different rates of return. This is a $100 monthly annuity. As shown in Figure 4 and Table 3, if $100 each month is allowed to grow at 6 percent, it will reach $46,204 in 20 years. Increase the rate of return to 12 percent, and the $100 each month for 20 years will be worth $98,926. Make that $100 payment each month for 35 years, and you will have $643,096!

Figure 4
Future Value of $100 a Month Invested

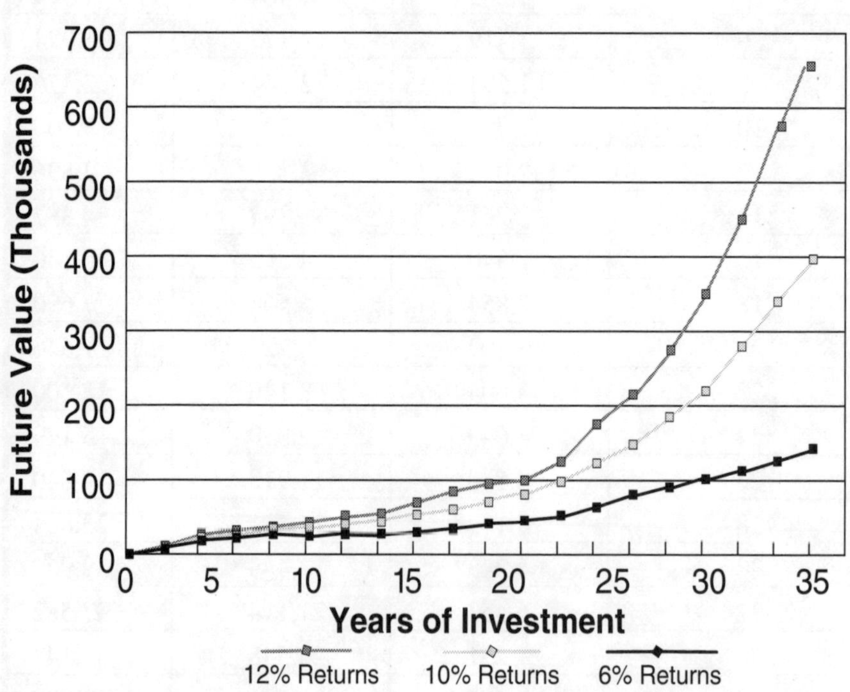

Table 3
Value of Compound Annuity of $100 per Month

	Annual Rate of Return		
	6%	10%	12%
Year	Value at End of the Year		
1	$ 1,234	$ 1,257	$ 1,268
2	2,543	2,645	2,697
4	5,410	5,872	6,122
6	8,641	9,811	10,471
8	12,283	14,618	15,993
10	16,388	20,484	23,004
12	21,015	27,644	31,906
14	26,230	36,381	43,210
16	32,109	47,044	57,562
18	38,735	60,056	75,786
20	46,204	75,937	98,926
22	54,623	95,317	128,307
24	64,112	118,969	165,613
26	74,807	147,834	212,981
28	86,863	183,059	273,127
30	100,452	226,049	349,496
32	115,768	268,513	446,465
34	133,032	342,539	569,589
36	142,471	379,664	643,096

SOURCE: Calculations by author. Amounts compound monthly; assumes that $100 is invested at the beginning of each month and the interest is allowed to accrue.

But if the monthly annuity is increased, then the amount that you will have increases just that much faster. The annuity concept is important in conserving for the down payment of a house, saving money for college, and preparing for retirement.

Do you think you can save $100 each month? How many families could easily afford to set aside $100 per month for 20 to 30 years in order to reap the benefits that would enhance the family's financial strength? With a consistent plan for setting funds aside and a carefully chosen rate of interest, the family can achieve some of its long-range financial goals through the power of compounding.

The Christian family can have enough funds to send children to college or to create a small estate of $226,049 by starting at age 35 and putting aside as little as $100 per month for 30 years, invested at 10 percent annual interest compounded monthly. The effects of taxes and inflation are not shown.

(Oh, the many couples who upon reaching retirement age wish they could have had the discipline to set aside funds on a regular basis!)

The Role of Taxes

"Render to Caesar the things that are Caesar's" (Mark 12:17, KJV). The things that are Caesar's are taxes. In our modern economy, the family may pay many forms of taxes:

- federal income taxes
- sales taxes
- state/local income taxes
- property taxes
- Social Security taxes
- excise taxes

In addition, there are hotel taxes, luxury taxes, gas-guzzling automobile taxes, personal property taxes, gift and estate taxes, gasoline taxes, and many others seemingly too numerous to mention.

These taxes affect financial planning because they affect the ability to purchase goods and services by changing *income* into *disposable income*:

DISPOSABLE INCOME = GROSS INCOME MINUS TAXES

Disposable income is the income after taxes.—In the fundamental relationship of financial management, when we speak of *income* we really mean *disposable* income. With this clarification in mind, it becomes clear that disposable income will be affected largely by how much is paid in taxes. The more money the family pays in taxes, the less money there is available to purchase goods and services or even to make contributions.

What is the difference between tax avoidance and tax evasion?—At this point it is useful to introduce two additional concepts: tax avoidance and tax evasion. Tax *avoidance* uses *legal* means to reduce the amount of taxes paid to the government. Tax *evasion* uses *illegal* means to reduce the amount of taxes paid to the government.

The Christian family will not evade the taxes required by a legally constituted government. However, the tax codes of the United States are structured to encourage tax avoidance, if the family wishes to do this.

Is there a moral issue involved in tax avoidance? That is, should the Christian family look for ways to avoid paying taxes? This question does not lend itself to easy answers. Perhaps some examples of tax avoidance will illustrate the principles involved:

- itemizing deductions, using the tax codes
- deducting charitable contributions from income
- giving away clothing, furniture, or other items of value and taking a tax write-off
- setting up a foundation in which the major purpose is to shield income from tax liability
- taking a tax loss on a business, in which the major purpose of the business is to shield income from tax liability

All these examples are instances of tax avoidance because they are legal means of reducing taxes. But for Christians all things legal are not necessarily morally acceptable behavior. Thus, in the matter of tax avoidance, Christians will carefully evaluate whether they are acting in ethically acceptable ways. And, of course, it may be necessary to get professional assistance in setting up tax situations that avoid taxes.

The purpose of tax avoidance is to decrease the family's tax liability by increasing legal exemptions and deductions. At any income level this will lead to larger amounts of disposable income. This is true for income designed for consumption purposes as well as income designed for estate planning. Failure to use ethically acceptable tax avoidance methods means that the Christian family transfers money *from* its own use *to* the use of the taxing authorities. A checklist of tax reduction efforts is shown in Exhibit 2.

Exhibit 2
Checklist of Tax Reduction Efforts

DECISION ITEM	YES	NO	ACTION NEEDED
Would the tax payment be smaller if the deductions were itemized?			
Do you need professional help with the tax computation?			
Have all permissible deductions been taken properly?			
Have all tax adjustments been taken properly?			
Are funds being set aside for retirement or the education of children in such a way that minimizes the tax liability?			
Has an individual retirement account or Keough retirement plan been established?			
Are investment losses or other allowable losses accounted for?			
Have all family deductions been taken?			
Have all taxes been properly calculated?			

Tax evasion, on the other hand, involves these types of activities:

- failing to file an income tax return
- deliberately omitting from the return income that is subject to taxation
- claiming more in deductions than should rightfully be claimed

Tax evasion is ethically and morally wrong. It could cause someone to go to jail!

How are taxes determined?—Taxes (tax liability) are the product of the applicable tax rate times the adjusted gross income minus the taxpayer's deductions.

TAXES = TAX RATE X (GROSS INCOME MINUS EXEMPTIONS MINUS DEDUCTIONS)

The federal tax system is progressively structured, which means that as the *gross income* level increases, the tax *rate* increases. Thus, a family with an annual gross income of $80,000 will usually pay taxes at a higher rate and have a greater tax liability than a family with an annual gross income of $20,000. Because of this, the *marginal tax rate* (the rate paid on the least amount of income) is a very important concept to understand.

What is a marginal tax rate?—Federal taxes due are calculated using a step process that involves marginal tax rates. The Internal Revenue Service (IRS) sets the tax rates for all single persons, married couples filing jointly, or married couples filing separately. Each taxable entity is assessed according to a schedule similar to the one shown in Exhibit 3 for married couple families.

Exhibit 3
Married Individuals Filing Joint Returns and Surviving Spouses for Tax Years Beginning in 1993

If taxable income is		The tax is	The marginal tax rate is	Of the amount over—
Over	but not over—			
$ 0	$36,900	———	+15%	$ 0
36,900	89,150	$ 5,535	+28%	36,900
89,150	140,000	20,165	+31%	89,150
140,000	250,000	35,928	+36%	140,000
250,000	———	75,528	+39.6%	250,000

SOURCE: Commerce Clearing House, Inc. 1993

The marginal tax rates are 15 percent, 28 percent, 31 percent, 36 percent, or 39.6 percent, depending on the tax bracket the family is in. The marginal rate means that for each additional dollar the family receives or pays out (if deductible), the family pays a tax of only 15 percent, 28 percent, or 31 percent of the amount received or paid out. Because the marginal tax rate is always less than 100 percent, it is not true that wage increases lead to less disposable income. *If you are offered a wage increase, take it.* Financially you will always be better off.

The *average tax rate* is the total tax liability divided by the total income. In addition to federal income tax, there are also Social Security taxes and state and local income taxes (in most states). The Social Security tax rate in 1992 was 7.65 percent of the first $55,000, whereas state income taxes ranged from 3 percent to 11 percent. When all these taxes are added together, the family with an adjusted income of $60,000 after deductions could face average taxes of 35 percent.

Table 4 illustrates how the gross income for a married couple family of four, with incomes of $25,000, $35,000, $50,000 and $100,000, is converted to disposable income.

Table 4
From Gross Income to Disposable Income

	Gross Income Amount			
TAX	$25,000	$35,000	$50,000	$100,000
Federal tax	2,000	4,129	6,087	15,180
State tax	1,190	1,960	2,700	4,900
Social Security tax	1,912	2,677	3,825	3,901
TOTAL TAXES PAID	$5,102	$8,766	$12,612	$23,981
DISPOSABLE INCOME	$19,898	$26,234	$37,388	$76,019

NOTE: To calculate the amounts on this table, several assumptions were made. These rates are for a married couple with two children. The federal rate assumes a standard deduction for the $25,000 and $35,000 incomes, a 25 percent deduction for the income of $50,000, and a 30 percent deduction for the $100,000 income. Social Security rates are 7.65 percent; and the state income tax rate is 7 percent of taxable income. The federal tax is from the 1991 schedule. Note that Social Security taxes are charged against gross incomes.

One of the practical results of the marginal tax system and the use of deductions to lessen taxes is that the true cost of deductible items such as charitable contributions will vary with the marginal tax rate faced by the family. That is:

COST OF CONTRIBUTIONS = (1 – MARGINAL TAX RATE) X CONTRIBUTION

Since there are only three marginal tax rates, it means that if the family is in the 15 percent marginal tax bracket, then every $1.00 of contribution costs only $.85 after deductions are taken. For the 28 percent tax bracket, the true cost of each $1.00 contribution is $.72. And for those at the 31 percent marginal tax bracket, the true cost is $.69. One consequence of this is that because of the progressive tax structure, those who have greater income are even better able to make charitable contributions.

These examples show the importance of giving careful consideration to the tax structure when doing financial planning. In the appropriate sections of this book, the impact of the tax structure will be examined to show how the Christian family can plan wisely.

Should the tithe be based on the gross or the net wages?—This question has intrigued Christians since the time that wage income started getting taxed (1913 in the U.S.). During the past century there was no national income tax, so there was no reason to think about gross income or net income. But in more modern times, the tax rates above are applied to gross income after deductions.

The family determines part of its tax rate by the types of expenditures it makes and by other aspects of its lifestyle. As a result, some—but not all—deductions are under the control of the family. Consequently, even though some taxes are under the control of the family, while other taxes are not, many return the tithe on the *gross* rather than on the *net* income. Table 5 offers a simplified illustration of the differences in tithing on the gross versus tithing on the net income.

If a family tithes the gross income, it may pay as much as 50 percent of its gross income in tithe (10 percent), offerings (5 percent), and taxes (35 percent). If they tithe on the *net* concept, the same family will pay far less in tithe. On the matter of tithing gross income versus net income, the Bible is silent. Most commentators suggest a simple 10 percent of the gross.

Table 5
Comparison of Tithe of Gross and Net Income

GROSS INCOME	AVERAGE TAX RATE	TITHE ON GROSS	TITHE ON NET
$ 25,000	20%	$ 2,500	$1,990
35,000	25	3,500	2,623
50,000	25	5,000	3,739
100,000	30	10,000	7,602

The Role of the Budget

A budget is a financial plan that shows the sources and amounts of income and how that income is spent on goods and services for a given period of time. When the budget is properly put together, it incorporates the fundamental relationship and all aspects of the economic environment.

Because the family budget is a means of satisfying the components of the fundamental relationship for a specified period of time, it may be structured for a month (probably the smallest practical time period for a budget), a half year, or a year. Budgets for time periods longer than one year require too much speculation about income and spending patterns to be useful. Such a budget really covers long-range planning, which may be useful only under special circumstances.

The budget is the basic tool of financial management for the Christian family. When properly developed, it takes into account inflation, interest, compounding, the time horizon, and the role of taxes. With the budget the family demonstrates its priorities, its philosophy regarding how it chooses to use its time as well as its money, and its attitude toward Christian stewardship. The budget is the one document to which all members of the family should contribute. It should be undertaken only after considerable prayer and much thinking.

The Bible places the budget into perspective when it raises the issue of whether those undertaking a venture have accurately counted its cost (Luke 14:28). Preparing a budget gives the family a systematic means of counting the cost. Like a beacon on a dark night, the budget can serve as a guide to help Christians achieve financial goals.

THE FAMILY BUDGET IS HOW THE FAMILY DISTRIBUTES ITS TOTAL INCOME.

There are no precise formulas for how the family should distribute its money. Each family must determine what works best for itself. However, there are certain guidelines on how much of any family budget should go toward the various categories of expenditures. For the Christian family it starts with the return of the tithe and the payment of offerings. Next comes the automatic tax that the federal government takes out. Shelter, food, clothing, transportation, savings, and miscellaneous items make up the bulk of the balance of the budget.

Table 6 and Figure 5 give an illustrative distribution of the major categories. This distribution suggests that 15 percent goes for tithes and offerings, 20-25 percent goes for taxes, and 25-30 percent goes for housing. But this is just a suggestion. Your family may have quite a different distribution. After you have read this book, you should have a much better idea of how to develop your budget.

Table 6
Illustrative Distribution of Family Income

Item	Low Income <$20,000	Moderate Income $20,000-$75,000	High Income >$75,000	Your Income/ Distribution
Tithes and Offerings	15%	15%	15%	
Taxes	20	25	25	
Housing	30	25	25	
Food	15	15	12	
Transportation	8	10	10	
Clothing	3	5	5	
Savings	2	3	3	
Miscellaneous	7	2	5	
TOTALS	100%	100%	100%	

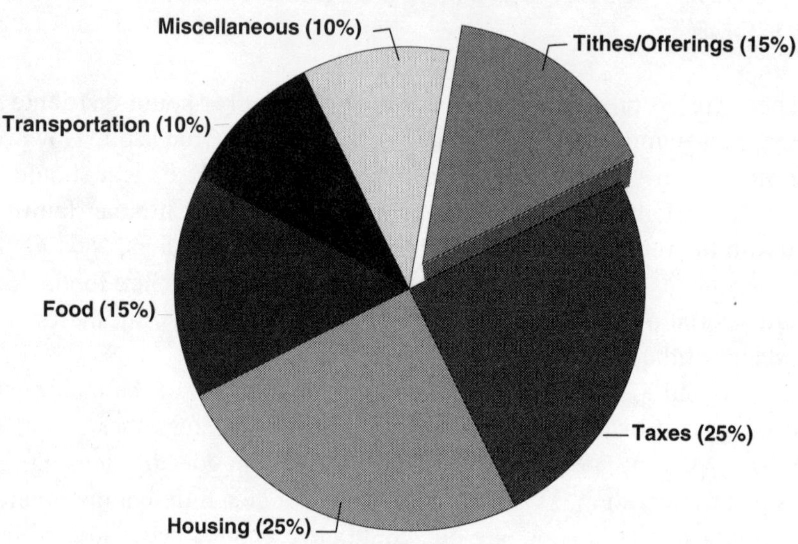

Summary

This chapter has introduced the economic environment that must be considered when the Christian family plans its finances. Successful use of these factors may help determine whether or not the Christian family achieves its financial-planning goals.

To use this section successfully, you should know what the following concepts mean:

- inflation
- compounding
- marginal taxes
- average taxes
- tax avoidance
- tax evasion
- interest
- returns
- CPI
- budget

You may wish to review how they are used in this chapter. Use them throughout the remainder of this book and as you plan your own finances.

3

Income and Its Sources

The word "income" does not appear in the King James Version of the Bible. The most frequently used word for what we call income is "increase," which appears more than 100 times. Usually the word "increase" is found in connection with harvest and natural output.

In Deuteronomy 14:28, KJV, the "increase" is the basis for setting the tithe. Whereas in biblical times the increase was measured in goods and less often in coins (coins were not invented until about 700 B.C.) or money, in the modern American economy the Christian family receives virtually all its increase in the form of money. The receipt of money income makes counting the increase much easier than finding the tithe on seven new cows, for example.

Sources of Family Income

Increase for the Christian family may conveniently be divided into the three sources of (1) wage and salary income, (2) nonwage income, and (3) government transfer payments.

TOTAL FAMILY INCOME = WAGE AND SALARY INCOME + NONWAGE INCOME + GOVERNMENT TRANSFER PAYMENT

Wage and salary income accounts for approximately 75 percent of the total income received by families in the United States. About 10 percent comes from nonwage income sources, and about 15 percent comes from government transfer payments. Each of these income sources will be discussed separately, with nonwage income discussed in the section involving investments.

Income From Wages and Salary

For most Christians, as is true for most American families, the major source of income is the wage and/or salary earnings of family members. The amount of such income varies by the number of family members who work, the wage rates of the working members, and the number of hours that each person works during a given week. The wage and salary earnings are computed as the sum of the income of the members of the family.

The sum of family earnings constitutes the gross earnings before taxes, and it may be the basis for determining how much tithe to pay. *Disposable earnings* are earnings after all taxes are paid. The amount of taxes paid, and therefore the disposable income available to the family, will vary with such factors as family size, pattern of spending, amount of deductible expenses, and the cost of living in the state and local area in which the family lives.

Another important factor is whether all family earnings are pooled. Generally the earnings of children are not considered when determining family income. However, the earnings of the working child help the child purchase things like clothes, which would otherwise come out of the family's budget.

The Working Wife and the Single Female Parent

The traditional family, consisting of two parents and children and the husband being the only source of wage earnings, is no longer the major type of family in the United States. Indeed, during 1992 in the United States, approximately one family in five had only one parent in the home. Currently more than 65 percent of all women work outside the home.

Data are not available on Christian families, but like society at large many Christian families have only one parent. When such a family situation exists, usually the children live with the mother. Unless the absent father provides adequate support—an event that occurs in only one separated family in three—the mother must work to support the family. If the Christian mother becomes a single parent, employment is often a necessity rather than a choice. The alternative is public support.

In two-parent families, the issue of whether or not the mother works outside the home depends on many things. For example, the presence, ages, and number of children are probably the most important factors. Some women choose to remain home with their children during the children's preschool years. For many Christian families, having the mother at home during the children's early years is the ideal.

Yet for many other two-parent families, the decision of whether or not the wife works is often determined by such things as the financial status that the family espouses, the wife's ability to earn respectable wages, and the wife's career aspirations.

The Christian wife and mother should consider the following when deciding whether or not to work outside the home:

- What will be the impact on the spiritual life of the children and the household?
- How will working outside the home affect the children?
- Are there reasonable alternatives to working outside the home?
- After accounting for all the costs of employment, is it economically sound to work outside the home?

Once these (and perhaps other) matters have been prayerfully and carefully decided, then she should make the decision.

Employment and Unemployment of the Christian Worker

Except for self-employed people, all workers will be employed by someone else and thus must periodically search for a job and run the risk of unemployment. For many workers, seeking employment presents serious problems. For others it is a routine matter that leads to immediate success.

Are there jobs that Christians should not seek? Is it permissible to be a lawyer? a banker? a police officer? For the Christian worker, the major concerns are with the moral and ethical issues involved with the job, the requirements for when work is to be performed, and the associations required in order to hold a particular job.

The ethical issue.—The basic question to be asked of any job or occupation is: Does doing this job in the way that it is normally performed cause conflict with the system of ethical beliefs that I hold as a Christian?

Those ethical beliefs include the proper keeping of the Sabbath, love for one's fellow humans, and adherence to all of the Ten Commandments.

If the answer to this question is an unequivocal no, then the job or occupation may be pursued.

The Sabbath work issue.—For many Adventist Christians there is a major concern about whether a job requires work on the Sabbath. This issue has largely been resolved for essential workers in Adventist institutions and for medical and emergency workers. For many others, however, a conflict remains. Even when there is essential work that has to be done on the Sabbath,

Christian workers must continually ask themselves what the absence from collective Sabbath worship is doing for their spiritual condition. Even if a job is considered essential and requires Sabbath employment, Christian workers may wish to avoid Sabbath work if their spirituality suffers as a result.

A more difficult problem occurs when a job requires only occasional Sabbath activity. This is typified by the job that requires an annual weekend-long meeting that the job holder is asked to attend. Does this once-in-a-while meeting really violate the precepts of the Sabbath?

The answer lies in the many experiences of the Bible characters. Temporizing often reveals the true condition of the heart and may lead to a breakdown of the meaningfulness of the Sabbath experience.

The questions that Christian workers must ask about any job performance include:

- Will it detract from my relationship with my God?
- Is it necessary that I have this job and not another?
- Are the duties of the job consistent with my beliefs?

The answers to these questions will determine whether there are requirements for a particular job so that the job should not be sought.

What about joining unions and associations?—Should Christian workers join trade unions? Some jobs require the workers to join a union or association as a condition of employment. This frequently poses a special dilemma for skilled workers, who more often than not are required to join a union. While Christians have many strong admonitions against joining the union movement, associations of white-collar workers seldom come under the same scrutiny. Yet many associations are in reality trade unions.

Should Christian workers join trade unions? In general, the advice is given to refrain from joining. However, the distinction is often blurred when there are associations that are not clearly the more traditional unions, such as professional societies that perform advocacy roles that are identical to those of the traditional trade unions.

Some of the central questions for Christian workers regarding unions are:

- Is it necessary to join a union or association in order to work at this job or perform this occupation?
- Are there alternative funding or support mechanisms that can be substituted for active participation in the union?
- Is the joining of the union or association consistent with my beliefs as a Christian?

The answers to these questions will help determine whether a union or association is joined, or even if the job is sought.

Coping with unemployment.—Into most lives a little unemployment will fall. Unemployment is not an unusual nor terminal condition. At any point in time one worker out of 12 is unemployed and looking for work. In the course of a year one worker in eight is likely to have a spell of voluntary or involuntary unemployment. The Christian family is not spared the problems associated with unemployment. Like other families, it must learn to adjust and cope.

If there are two parents in the household and both are wage earners, then the unemployment of one will be less financially troubling than if there is only one wage earner who becomes unemployed. In single-parent households, usually headed by a woman, unemployment can be devastating. In many such families the consequence can be public assistance. Job search problems are minimized if the family has set aside enough savings to cope with the rainy day that unemployment brings. The extent of family debt is another factor in how well the family will cope with unemployment.

Searching for a job.—Searching for a job is one of those activities that is at once frustrating yet rewarding if conducted properly. It is an essential part of the life of virtually every worker. Few workers have the luxury of having the job search for them, but some do. How one searches for a job will vary tremendously according to the age of the worker, his or her past experience, the level of education the worker has, whether or not the worker is just leaving college or graduate school, the wages one wants, and the occupation or job sought.

For example, each of the following persons would probably search for a job very differently:

- a teenager looking for his or her first job
- a housewife returning to work after raising a family
- a college graduate seeking a post-schooling job
- a business executive
- an experienced secretary
- an experienced steelworker after a plant shutdown

For some workers job search means preparing a résumé, distributing it, and waiting for the offers to come pouring in. For the vast majority of workers, however, job search usually is far more difficult. It involves using a process that is summarized by the six steps shown in Exhibit 5. These steps range from determining the type of job you are looking for to preparing for your next job by being a good employee on the present job that you have.

Exhibit 4
Steps in the Job Search Process

Step 1	*Determine* the type of job that you want to look for. This is often a function of what you have been trained to do or your previous experience. Research on what various jobs are like can be found at the library under *Occupational Outlook.* Write down the exact types of jobs you want.
Step 2	*Prepare* a résumé. It should contain the following vital elements: your name, address, and a telephone number where you can be reached. Your education should be highlighted, if that is a prominent feature of your background; otherewise, highlight your experience. Other aspects of résumé development can be found in the library.
Step 3	*Develop* a systematic means of looking for job vacancies. All or most of the following means should be used: —the public employment service —friends and relatives —direct personal contact with employers —school placement offices —newspapers' help-wanted ads
Step 4	*Prepare* carefully for job interviews by dressing correctly, knowing something about the job and the company, and having answers to basic questions, such as: Why do you want to work here? Can we contact your present employer? How you answer these questions during the interview will largely determine whether you get the job.
Step 5	*Follow up* on all contacts made by prospective employers. There should be a letter sent after an interview that concisely states why you should get the job. Continually review your search strategy and improve as necessary.
Step 6	*Prepare* for your next job by being an exceptional employee of the job that results from your search.

There are many excellent books in the library or the bookstore that help job searchers through all aspects of the job search process. These books can help you write a résumé, give you the names of companies and their chief officers, and provide information on letter writing and how to prepare yourself for job search. Use these types of books with the six steps shown here to assist you in your successful search.

What to do before you become unemployed.—If you are working, prepare for unemployment now! Start by being a good employee so that you will lessen the risk of being fired. Then take the following preventive steps:

- Periodically update your résumé or the portfolio of what you have been doing in your career.
- Start a rainy day savings fund to assist if you become unemployed.
- Periodically test the market to find out how much money is being offered by other employers for workers with skills like yours.
- Keep a list of potential future employers.

Once you believe that you will become unemployed, and even before you actually leave your old job, start the job search process aggressively, as outlined in Exhibit 4. File for unemployment insurance benefits, and let friends and relatives know that you are looking for a job. Assemble the materials that you will need for your search. By all means, do not go on vacation. There will be time for a vacation later. Remember the following rule of thumb regarding how long it will take you to be successful in your search.

IT WILL TAKE ABOUT ONE MONTH OF SEARCH FOR EVERY $10,000 PER YEAR IN INCOME THAT YOU WANT.

If you leave a job paying $50,000 per year, it will likely take you five months or longer to secure another one at the same level. How will you survive without income for that period of time? Unemployment insurance can help.

Unemployment insurance benefits.—Each state has established an unemployment insurance service in which unemployed workers may receive weekly benefits that range in excess of $250 per week and that lasts for as long as 26 weeks. The amount of benefits received and how long the worker receives benefits will depend on the worker's wage history, the reason the worker is unemployed, and the benefit schedule of the particular state in which the worker lives.

To receive unemployment insurance benefits, the worker must (1) apply for them at the local unemployment insurance office, (2) show that the unemployment was not because of his or her own actions (being fired for cause or quitting without good cause), (3) indicate a willingness and ability to work, and (4) actively search for a new job. Every week or two the unemployed worker must certify that he or she continues to be unemployed. Checks will be sent to the unemployed worker's home for as long as he or she is eligible.

FILE FOR UNEMPLOYMENT BENEFITS ON THE FIRST WORKING DAY AFTER THE OLD JOB ENDS, EVEN IF YOU DO NOT THINK YOU ARE ELIGIBLE.

Local unemployment insurance offices are found in every major city and county in the country. They are usually listed in the telephone book.

If the worker is not eligible for unemployment insurance benefits, he or she may actually be eligible for any one or more of numerous government programs designed to assist when individuals or families are in need.

Income From Cash and Noncash Government Benefit Programs

There are several types of government cash and noncash programs available to assist the family under a variety of circumstances when income from work is not available or is too small to support the family. These may be divided into "means-tested" programs and "employment-based" programs.

The means-tested programs are those that provide assistance when the family meets the eligibility requirements for assistance. This is always determined by the family's income.

The employment-based programs provide funds based on the individual's work history to those who meet the eligibility requirements. The requirements usually mean not having a job but looking for one or being retired.

Exhibit 5
Government Cash and Noncash Benefits

NAME	DESCRIPTION
Aid to Families With Dependent Children (AFDC)	This is the major support program for families with only one parent or with an unemployed parent and whose income is insufficient to meet daily necessities. The amount of the monthly aid will vary across states and with the size of the family.
Supplemental Security Income (SSI)	This program provides income for adults and children who are blind and totally disabled, and for adults over 65 who are destitute. Benefit amounts vary by circumstances.
General Welfare	This is a state-sponsored program for financially destitute single adults and families that do not qualify for other cash programs.
Food Stamps	A federally sponsored program in which eligible families or individuals receive free coupons that enable them to purchase food.
Medicaid	A federal-state program that provides medical benefit payments for eligible families and individuals.
Rental Housing Subsidies	An assortment of federal and state programs in which part of a family's rent payments are subsidized. The unit may be in a public housing unit or a privately owned rental house or apartment.

Should the Christian family accept welfare?—How should the Christian family react to these government programs? Are there ethical issues involved in accepting such government funds? Two concerns should govern the acceptance of such government funds by Christian families.

First, is there a real need for this source of income? Second, will the family develop a dependence on welfare that will erode the family's independence? The first question can be answered by a careful assessment of the family's immediate financial status. If reasonable alternatives are not available, then the family may find that the use of these government programs becomes a means of sustaining a minimum subsistence standard of living.

The second question is more difficult. Dependence occurs when the temporary nature of these programs is forgotten and the family comes to view welfare as permanent. For some families a permanent dependence can have debilitating effects on its feeling of self-worth and possibly on its spirituality. All efforts should be made to seek independence and self-sufficiency through training and employment. However, when self-sufficiency is not possible, the family should know that it need not feel any less loved of God because of those circumstances.

Calculating the Amount of Family Income

Sound financial planning requires each family to anticipate what income is available, the sources of that income, and the period or periods over which it expects to receive that income. To do this properly, we introduce the concept of *expected income*.

EXPECTED INCOME IS THAT INCOME THAT THE FAMILY HAS REASON TO EXPECT WILL COME ON A REGULAR BASIS AND IN AN AMOUNT THAT IS WELL KNOWN.

Expected income is to be contrasted with *transitory income*, such as an income tax return, an unexpected gift, a payment for special work, or other such income that comes infrequently. In setting up a financial plan, consider *only* expected income.

In some instances, the *actual income* received by the family is not the same as the expected income. The family made its plans on the basis of the expected income that it hopes to receive, but it spends only the income that it actually receives.

The concept of expected income is used because the family cannot know what income it will receive in the future. A family member may lose a job, get a pay raise, or experience any of a number of things that will change the amount of income received. However, for planning purposes it is helpful to plan using the expected income to reflect the uncertainty of the future.

In a similar manner, the financial plan should include the *expected taxes* that will be deducted from the expected income. This will provide the *expected disposable income* that will provide the basis for setting up the actual financial plan. In the next chapter when the budget plan is laid out, use the concept of the expected income and expected taxes.

The use of the concept of expected income also permits us to understand that there is nothing certain in this life. God alone knows what the future will be and what will become of us.

4

What Should You Spend Your Money On?

Much can be learned about a Christian family by the way it spends its income. For Christians, spending should result from two basic principles. The first is that God is the source of all we possess. The second is that all we do should glorify God (1 Cor. 10:31). These two principles mean that Christians will spend their money in ways that are notably different from the ways non-Christians spend their money. The differences in spending involve more than just the tithes and offerings given and the items purchased. They involve the whole of the spending pattern. First Corinthians 10:31 tells us that if we cannot glorify God in the way we spend money, then our spending is wrong!

There are very clear implications for frivolous spending or for spending on that which satisfies the lust of the flesh, the lust of the eyes, and the pride of life (1 John 2:16). I believe that if Christians truly examine much of what they spend money for, they would discover—pleasantly—that it is for that which ultimately does satisfy.

This chapter introduces spending and how to structure family spending so that it is in conformity with God's will as suggested by the two principles mentioned. It will place the emphasis on organizing the family's spending pattern so that it becomes clear what is going on.

Family Composition, Income, and Spending

Family composition will have a very strong effect on the spending pattern of the family. Although no two families are exactly alike and although spending patterns will vary across a number of factors (including family type and family income), we can identify basic groups into which most families will fall. Which family is yours?

The largest single group of families in this country are those families that have two parents and a middle-level income. In 1992 a lower-level income could be considered as one that was less than $20,000 a year; a middle level could be considered as that between $20,000 and $75,000 a year; and an upper income could be considered as that greater than $75,000 a year. Half of all families in the United States have incomes of less than $35,000 a year, and half have incomes that are greater than this amount.

Exhibit 6
Family Type and Distribution by Major Category

Family Type	Low Income <$20,000	Moderate Income $20,000-$75,000	High Income >$75,000
	Percent of all households		
One-adult household, with children	8.8	5.4	0.5
Two-parent household, with children	14.3	32.2	7.2
Over 65 household head	15.1	5.7	0.8
Single-person household	17.8	6.4	0.5

NOTE: The percentages will total more than 100 percent since some of the categories overlap.

SOURCE: *Money Income of Households, Families, and Persons in the Unites States: 1988 and 1989* (Bureau of the Census, U.S. Dept. of Commerce), Table 2.

There are many family composition types other than the middle-income, two-parent household. Many Christian families have only one parent in the home. In other Christian homes the children have grown up and gone away and the parents may be retired. No single spending pattern or budgeting plan will fit all 12 family types illustrated here. But there will be similarities within each family category.

As the coming sections proceed with the discussion of spending, each family should identify itself in one of the 12 categories and adjust its own budgetary habits accordingly.

Do You Know How to Establish a Budget?

Perhaps no single activity is more important to sound financial planning than establishing a budget for the family. *Every family has a budget.* At one extreme the budget is openly discussed with family members, prayed about, and then implemented. At the other extreme it is a haphazard, imprecise spending of whatever money is available. The first example certainly conforms better to God's will for financial soundness. The second type may leave the family without effective guidance in its financial affairs.

THE FIRST STEP IN PREPARING A BUDGET IS TO SET SHORT-TERM AND LONG-TERM GOALS FOR THE FAMILY.

Setting Goals for a Budget

The first step in creating a useful budget is to set a goal for family finances. This goal may be a short-term goal, that is, one that can be realized in a year or less. Or the goal may be a long-term goal for such things as saving for children's college education. As the goals change, the budget should change with it.

Examples of goals for a budget are:

- removing debt from the family
- financing a college education
- planning for retirement
- planning for a major vacation
- planning for a down payment for a house

Several aspects of these goals are worth noting. A goal may be set up for predictable time periods—such as the expected time for the start of college or of retirement. Or a goal may be for a fairly unspecified time period—such as when debt should be retired or when a vacation should be taken.

Of course, one goal may be somewhat mandatory for good financial management—such as planning for retirement—whereas another goal may be for something that is not essential but merely desired.

In setting goals the Christian family remembers Jesus' admonition:

"Seek ye first the kingdom of God, . . . and all these things shall be added unto you" (Matt. 6:33, KJV). When we remember God and keep in mind that our purpose for being on this earth is to give glory and honor to His name, then our goals will be honorable.

Setting Up the Budget

Use the information shown in Exhibit 7 to list all sources of income. The income should reflect permanent income only. (Do not include income that appears randomly.)

TO SET UP YOUR FAMILY BUDGET, LIST ALL INCOME AND POTENTIAL EXPENDITURES.

As shown in Exhibit 7, the budget should be set up for reasonable time periods, usually a month. In addition, it should show annual amounts. The monthly figures are used because that is the interval most often used to pay bills. The annual amounts are provided because they relate to annual tax periods and provide a perspective on how much income after taxes the family will have available.

Exhibit 7
Income From All Sources

Income Sources	Monthly Amount	Annual Amount
Wage and Salary Income		
Earnings of husband		
Earnings of wife		
Part-time earnings		
SUBTOTAL EARNINGS		
Earnings From Assets and Pension		
Pension or retirement		
Rental property		

Stock dividends		
Bond interest payments		
Mutual fund shares		
Royalties from books		
SUBTOTAL INCOME FROM ASSETS		
Income From Government Programs		
Social Security		
Workers' Compensation		
Unemployment Insurance		
Aid to Families With Dependent Children		
Supplemental Security Income		
General Welfare		
Income From Nongovernment Program		
Any Other Income		
TOTAL INCOME FROM ALL SOURCES		

How much of the family's income should it spend on shelter expenses? How much on family needs? How large a proportion of income will taxes take? Unfortunately, taxes are often determined for us. But even in this area the Christian family can ask how much it has to spend on federal, state, and local taxes.

These are some of the most difficult questions that the Christian family has to address when it seeks to determine how much to spend on each of the major spending categories. Exhibit 8 shows an illustrative distribution of the family's income into the seven major categories.

Exhibit 8
Expenditures of All Types

EXPENDITURE ITEM	MONTHLY AMOUNT	ANNUAL AMOUNT
TITHE AND OFFERINGS		
Tithe		
Offerings		
SUBTOTAL TITHE AND OFFERINGS		
SAVINGS		
INCOME TAXES		
Federal income		
Social Security		
State income		
SUBTOTAL INCOME TAXES		
HOUSING AND UTILITIES		
Mortgage/Rent		
Second mortgage		
Property taxes		
Property insurance		
Water and sewage		
Gas and electricity		
Periodic maintenance		
Other housing expenses		
SUBTOTAL HOUSING AND UTILITIES		
TRANSPORTATION COSTS		
Auto loan		
Periodic maintenance		
Public transportation		
Parking fees		

SUBTOTAL TRANSPORTATION		
CLOTHING AND HOUSEHOLD FURNISHINGS		
Clothing		
Furniture		
Household furnishings		
SUBTOTAL FURNISHINGS		
CREDIT AND CHARGE CARDS		
MasterCard		
Visa		
Department store cards		
Other cards		
Personal loans		
Credit union		
Other credit accounts		
SUBTOTAL CREDIT ACCOUNTS		
TOTAL ALL EXPENSES		

But, as has been stressed with regard to all other aspects of financial planning and money management, each family has to plan based on its own circumstances. Other than the 10 percent that is to be dedicated as tithe, there are no fixed amounts or percentages that the family should spend on any given category. However, there are many practical guides for prudent money management.

Your Income.—Once all income figures are included, you will know how much the family has to work with. This is very important. If you do not know how much income to expect, it is not likely that you will be able to prepare a proper budget. To get information on your annual income, check last year's tax statement, review your current check stubs, look at your financial records, and consult with your broker or lawyer. Include all sources of income.

Your Expenses.—Note that all potential expenses are included, including tithe, offerings, taxes, and savings. Two columns are included for expenses—*actual* expenses as reflected in your current status and *planned* expenses. The planned expenses are your way of taking charge of your spending and your financial life. The planned expenses are just as important as the actual, because they show the direction you want to go.

Tithes and Offerings.—Thousands of years ago Solomon admonished: "Honour the Lord with thy substance, and with the firstfruits of all thine increase" (Prov. 3:9, KJV). In the late twentieth century his words remain very good advice. Solomon and Malachi both suggest that temporal gain will come from such stewardship.

More important than even the temporal gain—be it crops, a new job, greater income, or whatever—it suggests a heart in tune with the great principle of stewardship. Stewardship begins with the recognition of God's ownership and God's gift to use the ability to acquire. From this perspective it is but a short step to recognizing God by returning to Him, through His instruments on earth, the means for the expansion of the gospel.

The Christian family recognizes that prudent stewardship—both of our money and our time—begins with God. But God has not left to chance how we are to be stewards. He says that the tithe, one tenth of our increase shall be "holy unto the Lord" (Lev. 27:30).

He asks that we bring the tithe into His storehouse. He does not compel us. It is only fitting that when the Christian family begins its spending decisions it should start with the tithe and offerings. After that, the balance of the family's income can be spent or saved in a manner that is most prudent given the family's goals, needs, and future objectives.

For the Christian family the tithes and offerings are gifts returned to God for His wonderful bountifulness. "Bring ye all the tithes into the storehouse" (Mal. 3:10, KJV). "Give unto the Lord the glory due unto his name: bring an offering, and come into his courts" (Ps. 96:8, KJV).

The tithe is 10 percent of our income (Gen. 28:22; Heb. 7:2, 4), and many Christians use the gross income as the basis for the tithe. (You'll recall that the gross income is the sum of all dollar income from all sources.)

Scripture does not define offerings as a certain percentage of our income, but they represent a liberal gift distinct and apart from the tithe. Each family must decide what portion of its income will be given as offerings.

Summary

This chapter has developed the basis for *spending*. It is important that the family understand well what its goals for spending are, what its resources are in the form of total income, and what its expenditures are. In addition, the family should use this opportunity to plan for future spending. This planning provides a means of getting control of your finances and of honoring God with your gifts.

In the sections that follow, we concentrate on three of the largest expenditures that the family is likely to make throughout a given period of time: spending for housing, transportation, and college education.

5

Where Should You Live and How Should You Pay for It?

One of the most important financial decisions that a family will make involves shelter. Most families will spend more for housing costs, in the form of a mortgage or rent payments, than for any other item. In thinking about shelter considerations, a sequence of decisions that the family will make has an impact on what those costs will be. This sequence includes the following decisions:

- Should the family buy a home or rent its housing?
- Should the family live in the central city, the suburbs, or a rural area?
- Should the family live close to its work or close to the school for its children?
- What percent of the family income should go for housing?
- When should the family buy its house, and how should it be financed?

Changes in the Family Circumstance Impact Housing

On average an American family moves every six years. Each time it moves it has to make some or all of the above decisions. And every time it moves, its circumstances change so that the decisions it makes may change. The notion of making one move into a house and staying there until the children are grown is no longer the way that the majority of families choose their housing.

Families grow and shrink, and their composition changes. With these changes come changes in housing needs. Not only do children come into the family and leave, but parents may separate and divorce, changing the housing needs. How is a family to make decisions regarding housing in light of all these potential changes?

A useful rule is: *Plan for the future as if you will be staying in one place for a relatively long time, but provide for the best "temporary" shelter because you may be there longer than you anticipate.*

The following rule of thumb will help you get the most out of your choice of housing.

PLAN YOUR HOUSING NEEDS FOR THE NEXT 15 YEARS, AND BE PREPARED TO STAY IN THAT HOUSE FOR THAT PERIOD OF TIME.

Should You Rent or Buy a House?

In 1990 about 59 million households owned or were buying a home, whereas about 36 million were renting. When families are able to afford it, most choose to buy their homes. The equity in a home represents the largest percentage of the net worth of most families. In most instances families that own homes are wealthier than families that do not, largely because of the equity in the homes.

Should the Christian family rent an apartment or house, or should it seek to buy a house? The answer is not easy or one that lends itself to automatic responses. Although the Christian family looks for the soon return of our Lord, it also heeds well the admonition given to the servants by the noble who went into a far country: "Occupy till I come" (Luke 19:13, KJV).

We do not know the time or the season when our Lord shall return, so prudence requires that in all ways we select the best use of the funds with which we have been entrusted. This includes paying for shelter.

The advantages of home ownership are many. The home, as the focal point of the Christian family's relationship to God and with each other, is one of the most precious places on earth. So interested is God in our home dwelling that Isaiah tells us that in the earth made new "they will build houses and dwell in them; they will plant vineyards and eat their fruit" (Isa. 65:21). Then, as if to underscore that there will be no renting in heaven, Isaiah says: "No longer will they build houses and others live in them" (verse 22).

Home ownership has both a romantic ideal and a practical attraction. But for many families the goal of home ownership is elusive and one that is outside their financial ability. All too often the decision to buy is made with only limited information about the true costs involved in this decision. It is often made on the basis of emotional factors that have little to do with the family's true needs. For example, a family may seek to purchase a house because it seems to be the "right" thing to do—that is, all families should own a house.

AN OWNER-OCCUPIED HOUSE IS A STORE OF WEALTH SINCE A HOUSE IS USUALLY AN APPRECIATED ASSET. AS THE HOUSE AGES, IT ADDS TO THE FAMILY'S NET WORTH LIKE FEW OTHER ASSETS DO.

Several factors should be taken into account before the family decides whether or not to buy. And given a decision to buy, the family has to determine how large a house to buy.

These factors include:

- the family's ability to buy (perhaps the most important factor)
- the age of the heads of the family
- the size of the family
- the age and educational needs of children
- the family's general financial condition

As an example of how important these factors are, consider the different housing needs of an elderly couple whose children are grown and have left the house in contrast with those needs of a family of two adults and three small children. The family with children will need a larger house—one able to accommodate growing, active children. The elderly couple may want space for entertainment.

Clearly, the particular circumstances of the family will largely influence whether to rent or buy. But by far the most important factor is whether or not the family can afford it. If in its current circumstances the family cannot afford to buy, renting becomes necessary.

Exhibit 9 lists several advantages and disadvantages of buying and renting. Each family must decide for itself just what the relative advantages and disadvantages are before deciding whether or not to buy a house. However, under most circumstances, if the family is able to afford the down payment and the monthly principal and interest payments, home ownership represents a far better financial move than perpetual renting. The financial advantages include the mortgage-interest tax deduction, increases in the value of the house (capital gain), and the use of a house as a store of wealth.

Exhibit 9
Advantages and Disadvantages of Renting and Buying

Advantages of Renting	Advantages of Buying
Less money outlay	Builds equity
Can easily move to another location	Permanence of housing services
No need to incur maintenance costs	Ability to write off the interest and property tax payments
Housing size can easily adjust to changes in family size	Once you buy a house, it is easier to buy another
No property or other taxes to incur	Generally larger space
Disadvantages of Renting	**Disadvantages of Buying**
Lack of equity	Large outlays for maintenance and upkeep
No tax advantage	May not be easy to sell
May be forced to move because of ownership changes	Need to have large down payment
No control over external conditions around property	May incur loss if housing prices decline

Where Should the Family Live?

The United States is a vast nation with a divergent array of cities, urban centers, suburbs, rural communities, and farm areas. More than 75 percent of the 250 million people living in the United States dwell in urban centers. As recently as 70 years ago, most residents lived in rural areas. Many people settle in the section of the country in which they grew up, or in places that are of interest to them, or in places that provide the type of jobs they need, or in places in which a combination of circumstances cause them to locate.

For many Christian families the decision to live in central cities, suburban centers, or rural communities depends on the total environment desired for the family and the family's ability to finance living in this environment. The desired environment often includes employment opportunities, schools, churches, and the social/cultural activities of the area. Each family must choose the mix that it feels is important for its development, nurturing, and maturity. It is not clear whether one living condition offers a superior arrangement, for all families, over another. Each family must consider which combination of these factors best meets its overall needs and financial ability.

During this century there have been profound changes in transportation and communications. As a result fewer people are forced to live close to where they work or even where they want their children to attend school. It is not at all uncommon for workers to travel 40 to 50 miles each way to work. Before the advent of interstate highways and high-speed automobiles such commuting patterns were not practical.

The location of appropriate schooling for children is an important factor in the choice of where to live. This decision can be instrumental in the overall financial structure of the family. For example, if a family chooses to live in an area in which Christian schooling is not available, it may be faced with more expensive boarding schools for its older children if it wants them to receive a Christian education.

In summary, the choice of where to live involves many factors, not the least of which are:

- the family's view on the type of environment it feels is most conductive to the spiritual benefit of the family
- the costs involved in living in various parts of the community
- the amount of commuting to jobs the workers of the family are willing to tolerate
- the availability of Christian education
- the family's income

All these issues must be prayerfully considered.

How Much Does Housing Cost?

Housing expenses vary from the simplest public housing rental unit that may cost $100 a month to the most expensive mansion costing millions of dollars, and to practically everything in between. Table 7 lists 1991 median rent and housing costs in the major sections of the country. How much *you* pay, however, will still vary with the quality of your housing, the area you live in, and your particular housing demands.

It is clearly more expensive to live in the Northeast than in the Midwest. Nonetheless, in areas in which housing is more expensive, salaries and wages are often (but not always) higher.

In 1991 the national median sale price of a house was $120,000. Half the houses sold in the country cost more, and half cost less. Some regions of the country, like the East, had median sale prices well in excess of $150,000. Other regions, like the South, had median prices at $100,000. However, in each region of the country housing costs will vary greatly, depending on where the house is located, what amenities it has, and how large it is. Median sale prices were as high as $256,600 in the San Francisco, California, area and as low as $68,500 in Des Moines, Iowa.

Table 7
Median Rents and Housing Costs Across Regions of the Country

Area	Median Rents	Median Prices for New Houses
Northeast	$432	$155,400
Midwest	$319	$110,000
South	$324	$100,000
West	$473	$142,300
United States	$374	$120,000

SOURCE: *Statistical Abstract of the United States* (U.S. Government Printing Office, 1991), Table 1215.

Under most conditions, for similar housing the costs are greater in the cities than in the more remote small towns and rural areas. Rents, like housing prices, tended to be higher in the Northeast and lower in the Midwest. It all depends on where you live.

How Much Should You Pay for Your House?

This question has two parts: (1) How much should you pay to buy or rent a particular house, and (2) how much of your income should you devote to housing costs? Is there such a thing as an extravagant house? Of course. When the Christian family seeks to buy a house, it should not look for a house that will entail such an expense as to leave it financially exhausted and depleted. Many a family has regretted purchasing a house that has left it in dire financial straits if one member of the household loses a job. Worse yet is purchasing a house whose cost will leave the family unable to fulfill its financial obligations to return a faithful tithe and to give offerings.

In choosing how much to spend on a house, remember to stay within your financial ability. As we will see later, that usually means that your household expenses should not exceed 25 to 30 percent of your monthly income.

Negotiating a purchase price.—The market for *all* houses is a bargaining market. Even when a developer offers several houses for sale in a development and lists their prices, this is nothing more than the "ask" price. You have the right to submit a "bid" price that is lower than the asking price. More frequently than you can imagine, the developer will accept your bid or will negotiate a price that is actually lower than the original asking price. You have nothing to lose by offering a lower price.

To be effective in these type of negotiations, develop a feeling for whether housing prices are increasing or decreasing in a particular area. In a market of declining house prices, the seller may be very happy to accept your lower bid. In a market of rising house prices, the seller may decline your offer. But that is a risk worth taking in order to save yourself potentially thousands of dollars.

ALWAYS OFFER AS YOUR "BID" PRICE A LOWER PRICE THAN THE "ASK" PRICE OF THE PERSON OR COMPANY SELLING THE HOUSE.

Negotiating a rent.—There usually isn't much room for negotiating when a rental is involved. However, you can ask for certain amenities such as new paint, a refurbished bath, a new refrigerator, or other such items. If you rent in an area in which there is a glut (excess number of units), you may want to explore the idea of several months of free rent in exchange for a longer lease. If the market is really glutted, you may get concessions that will permit you to rent a larger or more suitable unit for the same amount of money. It's up to you to shop wisely.

TO AS LARGE AN EXTENT AS POSSIBLE, THE FAMILY SHOULD NOT PAY MORE THAN 30 PERCENT OF ITS MONTHLY INCOME ON HOUSING EXPENSES.

How much of your income should go for housing?—The answer may surprise you. The family that is renting, on average, spends 29 percent of its income on monthly housing costs. The family that is buying spends 18 percent of its income. Renters tend to have lower incomes than buyers and tend to pay a much greater percentage of their income on housing. About one third of all renters pay more than 40 percent of their monthly income on housing costs. Recent buyers, however, tend to pay about 30 percent of their monthly income on housing costs.

Mortgage payments become smaller part of family income.—Home ownership, under provisions of a fixed 30-year mortgage, means that as long as the family remains in the same house (and doesn't refinance the house), the family will not experience an increase in its principal and interest payments over time. However, the family that is renting is likely to see a steady increase in rent payments. In contrast, over time the family that stays in the same house will likely pay a smaller and smaller percent of its income on housing.

What Are the Costs Associated With Buying a House?

Buying a house requires that a family be able to pay the principal and interest of the mortgage (of course, if the family pays cash there will be no mortgage), property taxes, homeowner insurance, and general maintenance costs. In addition, the family must provide a down payment that can easily exceed 10 to 20 percent of the sale price of the house.

Except for maintenance costs, some of the approximate costs of home ownership are illustrated in Table 8. Four houses costing four different prices are chosen for this illustration: $80,000, $100,000, $150,000, and $200,000. This price range spans the average sales price of a house in most regions of the country.

Although many lenders would like for you to pay 20 percent as a down payment on a house, there are options for lower payments:

- If you are a veteran, you can pay nothing down.
- If your home is insured under the Federal Housing Association, your down payment can be as low as 5 percent of the value of the house.
- You can always ask for a lower required down payment; you just might get it.

The information in Table 8 shows that if the family wishes to buy a house costing $100,000, it will need $20,000 as a down payment, have a monthly principal and interest payment of $805, have monthly property taxes and insurance costs of $300, and will need a minimum of $53,000 in annual income. The family should not have more than $14,850 in total debt from all other sources. If the house increases in value to $200,000, the family will need an annual income of $106,000.

Table 8
Approximate Costs of Home Ownership

Price	$80,000	$100,000	$150,000	$200,000
Down Payment (20%)	$16,000	$20,000	$30,000	$40,000
Monthly Principal and Interest (9%)	644	805	1,207	1,609
Monthly Property Taxes/Insurance (3%)	240	300	450	600
Total Monthly Costs	884	1,105	1,657	2,209
Required Monthly Income	$3,536	$4,420	$6,628	$8,836
Maximum Amount of Total Debt	$11,900	$14,850	$22,270	$29,690
Required Annual Income	$42,432	$53,040	$79,536	$106,032

NOTE: This table assumes that there will be a 20 percent down payment and that the balance will be financed at 9 percent interest per year for 30 years. It also assumes that the monthly property taxes and insurance are 3 percent of the total price of the house. The required monthly income is 4 times the monthly housing costs. Total debt is not to exceed 28 percent of the annual income.

Clearly the annual income required is about three and a half to four times the amount of the annual costs of housing. When interest rates are higher, the monthly costs will increase above those shown here. For homes priced higher than $200,000 the relative costs can be approximated by combining any two columns. The use of three and a half to four times is just about what most banks and mortgage finance companies will require before approving a loan. In addition, most loan companies will require that the total of all other debts (outside of the mortgage) be less than 30 percent of the annual income.

Table 9 lists the approximate monthly interest and principal figures for 30-year financing of amounts ranging from $60,000 to $300,000 at interest rates ranging from 6 percent to 12 percent. Find your approximate monthly mortgage payment on this table. You can also get some idea of what a mortgage will cost you at different interest rates and different amounts financed.

Table 9
Calculation of Mortgage Amounts

INT.	Amount Financed												
RATE	60,000	80,000	100,000	120,000	140,000	160,000	180,000	200,000	220,000	240,000	260,000	280,000	300,000
	Monthly Payments of Principle and Interest												
6.00	360	480	600	719	839	959	1,079	1,199	1,319	1,439	1,559	1,679	1,799
6.25	369	493	616	739	862	985	1,108	1,231	1,355	1,478	1,601	1,724	1,847
6.50	379	506	632	758	885	1,011	1,138	1,264	1,391	1,517	1,643	1,770	1,896
6.75	389	519	649	778	908	1,038	1,167	1,297	1,427	1,557	1,686	1,816	1,946
7.00	399	532	665	798	931	1,064	1,198	1,331	1,464	1,597	1,730	1,863	1,996
7.25	409	546	682	819	955	1,091	1,228	1,364	1,501	1,637	1,774	1,910	2,047
7.50	420	559	699	839	979	1,119	1,259	1,398	1,538	1,678	1,818	1,958	2,098
7.75	430	573	716	860	1,003	1,146	1,290	1,433	1,576	1,719	1,863	2,006	2,149
8.00	440	587	734	881	1,027	1,174	1,321	1,468	1,614	1,761	1,908	2,055	2,201
8.25	451	601	751	902	1,052	1,202	1,352	1,503	1,653	1,803	1,953	2,104	2,254
8.50	461	615	769	923	1,076	1,230	1,384	1,538	1,692	1,845	1,999	2,153	2,307
8.75	472	629	787	944	1,101	1,259	1,416	1,573	1,731	1,888	2,045	2,203	2,360
9.00	483	644	805	966	1,126	1,287	1,448	1,609	1,770	1,931	2,092	2,253	2,414
9.25	494	658	823	987	1,152	1,316	1,481	1,645	1,810	1,974	2,139	2,303	2,468
9.50	505	673	841	1,009	1,177	1,345	1,514	1,682	1,850	2,018	2,186	2,345	2,523
9.75	515	687	859	1,031	1,203	1,375	1,546	1,718	1,890	2,062	2,234	2,406	2,577
10.00	527	702	878	1,053	1,229	1,404	1,580	1,755	1,931	2,106	2,282	2,457	2,633
10.25	538	717	896	1,075	1,255	1,434	1,613	1,792	1,971	2,151	2,330	2,509	2,688
10.50	549	732	915	1,098	1,281	1,464	1,647	1,829	2,012	2,195	2,378	2,561	2,744
10.75	560	747	933	1,120	1,307	1,494	1,680	1,867	2,054	2,240	2,427	2,614	2,800
11.00	571	762	952	1,143	1,333	1,524	1,714	1,905	2,095	2,286	2,476	2,667	2,857
11.25	583	777	971	1,166	1,360	1,554	1,748	1,943	2,137	2,331	2,525	2,720	2,914
11.50	594	792	990	1,188	1,386	1,584	1,783	1,981	2,179	2,377	2,575	2,773	2,971
11.75	606	808	1,009	1,211	1,413	1,615	1,817	2,019	2,221	2,423	2,624	2,826	3,028
12.00	617	823	1,029	1,234	1,440	1,646	1,852	2,057	2,263	2,469	2,674	2,880	3,086

What are points?—A "point" associated with a house is 1 percent of the cost of a house. Thus, if you are contemplating buying a house that costs $200,000 and the lender will charge three points for closing costs, then the closing costs are $6,000 ($200,000 x .03 = $6,000). You will sometimes see the costs listed as separate charges that may be included in the overall price of the house. In many instances, these points are negotiable. You should examine carefully what points are being charged for the house you are buying.

Where will the down payment come from?—Obtaining enough money for the down payment is frequently the biggest obstacle to home purchase. When a 20 percent down payment is required, the family is often unable to save fast enough to produce it.

For the least costly house on the list, $16,000 cash is required for a 20 percent down payment. However, if a lower down payment is accepted, the mortgage payment will be higher. For some Christian families the lower down payment and the higher mortgage payment may be the only way they will be able to afford to buy a house.

Sources of income for the down payment include:

- funds obtained from the sale of a previously owned house
- money saved over time
- money borrowed from friends or relatives
- money obtained from cashing out other assets

The seller of the house is also a potential source of some of the down payment. The seller may be persuaded to hold a second mortgage for part or all of a down payment. In some instances, when a young couple both work, they may decide to live on one salary so that they can save virtually all the other for a down payment.

FEW BANKS OR LENDING INSTITUTIONS WILL APPROVE A MORTGAGE IN WHICH THE FAMILY HAS BORROWED THE MONEY FOR THE DOWN PAYMENT.

An alternate route is to buy a smaller house that can be expanded or renovated to meet the needs of the family. However it is done, the Christian family often has to use a creative solution to one of the basic problems in modern life.

The Amount Financed

Few families are in a position to pay cash for a house, and even if they were there are many financial disadvantages to doing so. Therefore, for virtually all Christian families, financing a house will be the normal way to home ownership. Once a house price is settled on, the amount of the down payment will determine the amount financed. The interest rate charged for that amount will then determine the monthly payments made by the family. Since the amount the family will be able to pay is related to the family's income, the amount to be financed and the monthly mortgage costs are an important part of the decision whether or not to buy a house. For many families the monthly mortgage payment is as important as the amount financed.

Partition of the monthly payment into principal and interest.—The 30-year, fixed-term, fixed-interest rate mortgage is the most popular type of mortgage. The interest rate is fixed, and there are equal monthly payments of principal and interest until the debt is paid in full. As incomes go up, the note becomes easier to bear.

A fixed-rate mortgage remains the same in absolute dollar amounts for the life of the loan. However, the monthly amount is partitioned into the repayment of the principal and the monthly interest charge. In the early years of a loan the interest portion represents a substantial amount of the monthly payment. As the loan matures, the interest becomes a smaller portion and the principal repayment gets larger.

Figure 6 illustrates this concept. In Figure 6 a 30-year $100,000 mortgage at 10 percent is separated into the principal and interest payments for each of the 30 years. The monthly principal and interest is $877.57. During the first year $44.24 goes toward the principal and $833.33 goes into interest payments. By year 10, $118.77 goes toward the principal and $758.81 into interest. (The principal is not declining very quickly, is it?) At that time the principal remaining is $90,519. It is not until about year 23 that the same amount goes into principal and interest. At that time the principal remaining is $50,681. Only after year 23 does the remaining principal rapidly decline.

What about a 15-year mortgage?—A most remarkable thing happens when the mortgage extends for only 15 years instead of 30 years—the family saves thousands and thousands of dollars with only a small increase in the monthly principal and interest payment. A family that finances a $100,000 mortgage for 15 years instead of 30 years can realize $122,497 in lower total payments during the life of the mortgage! If the family finances $200,000, the amount saved is $244,994. These savings take into account the higher amount paid out each month for a 15-year mortgage. Look at the savings shown in Table 10.

Table 10
Comparisons of 15- and 30-Year Mortgages

Amount Financed	30-Year Mortgage	15-Year Mortgage	Difference in Monthly Payment	Difference in Total Payments	Net Savings
	Monthly Principle and Interest				
$ 60,000	$ 527	$ 645	$118	$ 73,498	$24,499
80,000	702	860	158	97,997	32,666
100,000	878	1,075	197	122,497	40,832
120,000	1,053	1,290	237	146,996	48,999
140,000	1,229	1,504	275	171,496	57,165
160,000	1,404	1,719	315	195,995	65,332
180,000	1,580	1,934	354	220,494	73,498
200,000	1,755	2,149	394	244,994	81,665
220,000	1,931	2,364	433	269,493	89,831
240,000	2,106	2,579	473	293,992	97,997

NOTE: The monthly mortgage figures use a 10 percent annual interest rate. The difference in total payments is the difference over the life of the mortgage—15 years for the 15-year mortgage and 30 years for the 30-year mortgage. To get the net savings, the difference in payments are invested at 10 percent for 15 years, and the returns subtracted from the difference in total payments. All numbers are rounded to the nearest dollar.

A 15-YEAR MORTGAGE AT THE SAME OR A SLIGHTLY HIGHER RATE THAN A 30-YEAR MORTGAGE IS ALMOST *ALWAYS* A SUPERIOR WAY TO BUY A HOUSE.

Only two caveats are in order. First, by paying a larger amount, the family may need to buy a house costing less if its income cannot support the higher mortgage. Second, the ability to invest the difference may vary.

The savings just shown occur because of the nature of the amortization process. With the mortgage being paid off in just 15 years, the principal declines at a faster rate and the family ends up paying far less interest charges. There is nothing magical about these figures. However, in almost every case there would still be tens of thousands of dollars saved.

For an illustration why the 15-year mortgage is usually superior, take a look at Figure 7 for the 15-year $100,000 mortgage at 10 percent. The total monthly principal and interest is $1,075, but the amount that goes toward interest in the first month is $833.33—the same interest as in the 30-year mortgage. The amount that goes toward principle is $241.27. As Figure 7 shows, the higher payments mean that within eight years approximately the same amount goes for principal and interest. After that, more of the payment goes toward the remaining principal. When you compare Figures 6 and 7, you can clearly see why the 15-year mortgage is usually superior.

Figure 6
Principal and Interest Portions of Monthly Payment

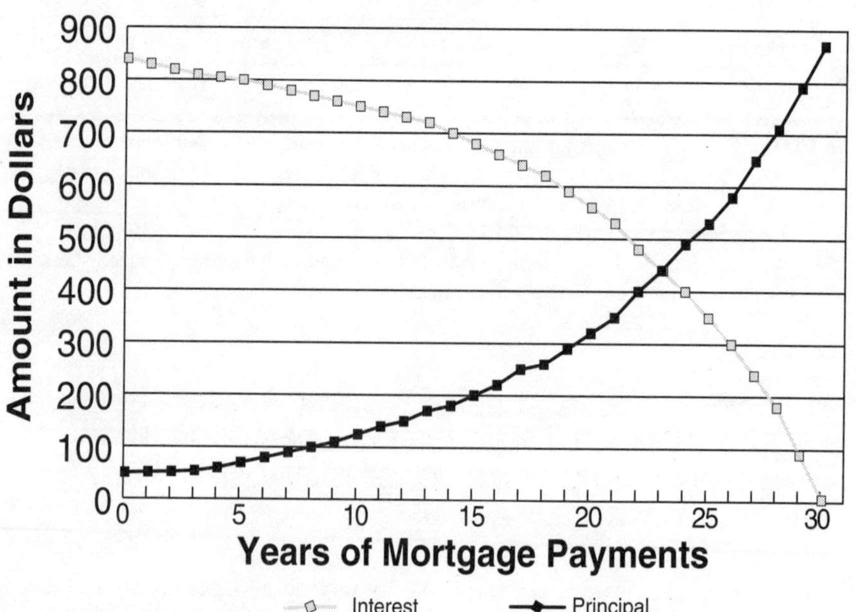

Figure 7
Principal and Interest Portions of Monthly Payment

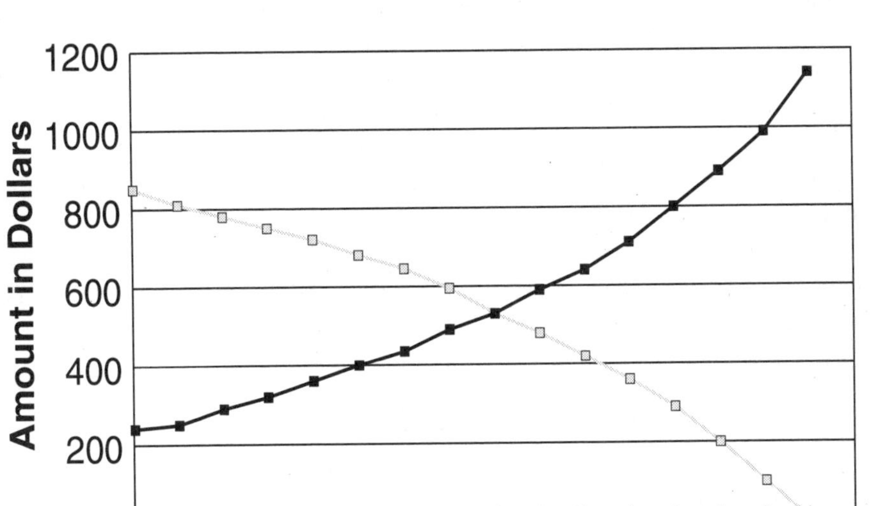

Interest payments and tax write-offs.—Since interest payments are deductible from income when tax payments are calculated, large interest payments are subsidized by the tax code. For example, if a family is paying $640 interest on a $658 monthly mortgage payment, at different marginal tax rates the family actually pays far less. The formula for this is:

COST OF MORTAGE = [(1 – MTR) X INTEREST CHARGE] + PRINCIPAL

This formula shows the true cost of the mortgage depends on the family's marginal tax rate (MTR). Thus, from the formula it is clear that although a monthly mortgage interest payment may be $658, after the interest is deducted from income taxes the cost of the mortgage is only $461 at the 28 percent marginal tax rate. It is this subsidy of the interest payment that makes home ownership a more attractive financial decision than is immediately obvious.

Monthly property taxes and insurance.—Taxes on property and any insurance costs are usually paid semiannually, but for purposes of understanding how they relate to the total family budget, it is useful to show these amounts as monthly payments. In the illustration in Table 8 above, it is suggested that these payments are 3 percent of the total price of the house. However, the prudent prospective homeowner should know what the property tax and insurance charges are likely to be, because they may vary tremendously across states and within jurisdictions within any given state.

Property taxes are deductible from federal income taxes. And just as we have seen for interest payments, the net cost of the monthly property tax charge to the family will be much less, depending on the marginal tax rate of the family.

Financing Your House

Whether you use a 30-year fixed-rate mortgage (which is still the most popular way to finance your house), a 15-year mortgage, or another type of mortgage, it will be insured under conventional, federal, or veterans' loan provisions.

The Federal Housing Administration (FHA) and Veterans Administration (VA) loans have permitted millions of American families to finance their houses when they would not otherwise qualify for a conventional loan. If you are a military veteran, you should take advantage of a VA loan that permits your family to become homeowners. If your income is relatively low, then an FHA guaranteed loan may be possible for you. Because of these programs, there are alternative opportunities for families to become homeowners. See Table 11.

Alternative Financing Methods

As interest rates have increased and as there has been a declining availability of conventional fixed-interest long-term mortgages, many families have sought alternative ways to finance their homes. The purpose of these alternatives is to permit the family to qualify for a higher mortgage loan than their current income would normally permit.

For example, if the family's income is $40,000 per year, they may not find a house of the size and in the neighborhood that they want and can afford under conventional fixed-term rates. Instead they may need to finance the house in such a way that the monthly payments are low during the early years of the loan when their income is smaller. To make this type of arrangement attractive to the lender, the interest rate or loan payments must later go up to accommodate the early lower rate. This can lead to creative financing methods.

CREATIVE FINANCING INVOLVES A METHOD OF LOWERING THE REQUIRED MORTGAGE PAYMENT EARLY IN THE LOAN PERIOD, BUT COMPENSATING LATER WITH HIGHER OR LONGER PAYMENTS WHEN THE FAMILY'S INCOME HAS INCREASED.

Table 11
Major Features of Types of Mortgage Loans

	TYPE OF LOAN		
MAJOR FEATURES	CONVENTIONAL	FEDERAL	VETERANS
Loan Limits	None	Varies with locale, but not more than $204,000	Not to exceed $204,000
Guarantee Agency in Case of Default	Varies; contracts usually sold on the secondary market	Federal Housing Administration	Veterans Administration
Required Down Payment	Usually 20% of purchase price	At least 5% of of purchase price	Usually no money down
Special Qualifications	Higher income and credit requirements	Limit on the amount of income the family can have	Must be a veteran of the U.S. military

Creative financing plans will permit the family to buy a house that they could not afford under conventional financing, but they can involve far more risk for the family. To understand why, let us examine several of the more popular creative financing plans.

Flexible-rate mortgage.—A flexible-rate mortgage—also called an adjustable-rate mortgage (ARM)—is one in which the interest rate charged on the loan will vary with a known indicator, such as the interest rate charged on six-month Treasury bills or on three-year Treasury notes. If these interest rates go up, the interest charged on the mortgage and the monthly mortgage will also increase. To induce families to accept such uncertainties, the initial interest rates are almost always a point or two lower than existing rates.

To keep adjustable rates from fluctuating too much, the loan may come with an interest rate cap or a payment cap. Under a periodic *interest rate cap*, there is a limit to the amount that interest rates can increase at any one time. There may also be an aggregate cap that limits the total amount that the interest rate can go up throughout the life of the loan.

A *payment cap* places a limit on the amount of the monthly mortgage and interest payment, even if interest rates go up. The lender will make up for lost interest by reducing the amount of the monthly payment that is applied to principal. The net result is that under a payment cap as interest rates go up, the amount paid on principal goes down and the length of the payment period increases.

In the extreme, when interest rates go up high enough, the monthly payment does not cover even the interest charges. The lender adds the unpaid interest to the remaining principal. The result is that the family has a declining equity in their home even though they are continuing to make monthly payments.

Graduated-payment mortgage.—Graduated-payment mortgages (GPMs) are designed for homeowners who expect to be able to make larger monthly payments in the near future. During the early years of the loan, payments are relatively low, but are structured to rise at a set rate over a set period of time. Interest rates are fixed so that the difference between what the family should pay and what it is actually paying is made up by higher payments later.

Under a GPM the family knows exactly how frequently the monthly payment will increase and the amount of the increase. The family anticipates that increased income will permit it to make the higher payments later.

However, if there are financial reverses or if the income does not materialize, the family could find itself in greater debt than it can reasonably manage.

Balloon mortgage.—A balloon mortgage has monthly payments based on a fixed interest rate. However, payments are usually for a very short period of time—usually three to five years—and at the end of that time the full amount of the loan is due in one balloon payment. The monthly payments are often for interest only, so they are lower than would be true of conventional loans. At the end of the loan period the mortgage is refinanced, the single payment to retire the debt is paid, or the property is sold.

Under this payment plan the family expects to be able to refinance in a way that permits home ownership. The real danger is that when the balloon payment is due the family may not be able to obtain new financing (this could occur because of unemployment or some financial reverses). The house may then have to be sold under very unfavorable conditions. The net result could be that the family loses all its investment in the property. This is a very risky type of loan.

Seller take-back.—Under this plan the seller of the house provides some of the financing under a first or second mortgage. The plan can be structured to meet the needs of both seller and buyer. For example, if the price of a house is $100,000, the family puts down $20,000 and then borrows $60,000 from a conventional lender. This is a first mortgage. The seller then "lends" the family the remaining $20,000 to make up the total cost of the house. This is the second mortgage. The terms are then agreed upon for the second mortgage, but usually it is for a much shorter term than the first mortgage and may include a balloon payment.

The advantage of this plan is that the family will have a much lower first mortgage and will have several years to arrange to get the balloon payment of the second mortgage. However, the holder of the second mortgage has the right to foreclose in the event of default. The family may not be able to make the balloon payment at the end of the second mortgage period, thus being forced to sell the house or lose the entire investment.

Other creative financing plans.—There are many other creative financing plans available that permit home ownership at a rate that a family can afford. However, the Christian family is admonished to be wary of these plans. All carry the risk that later on the family will have to make up for the smaller payments made during the early life of the loan. They may also provide a false sense of affordability of the house. In all such endeavors, the

Christian family is warned to consider the cost before venturing into any long-term debt. If the cost is too high, then avoid the commitment.

Which Financing Plan Is Best for Your Family?

In this chapter we have examined many ways to finance the purchase of a home. The financing method that is the best for you depends on your personal circumstance. *The 15-year fixed-interest rate loan is the financing method that offers the least total payments and that has the least risk.* If mortgage interest rates are high, say 10 percent, then an adjustable mortgage—an ARM—may have some attractive features. If you anticipate a dramatic increase in income during the next few years, then you may want to consider one of the alternative financing methods.

It should be noted, however, that there may be increased risks if the anticipated income does not materialize or if the interest rates suddenly increase dramatically. Prudent financial planning may require that the Christian family finance the home in the way that seeks to reduce the risks of home ownership.

Should You Refinance Your Home?

Should you pay off the old loan and take out another?—In 1980 mortgage interest rates reached as much as 17 percent. By late 1993, rates were as low as 4.5 percent on ARM financing and 6 percent on a 30-year, fixed mortgage. Should families that financed at 17 percent refinance when the interest rates hit 8 percent? Well, that depends. Refinancing under favorable conditions *will* result in lower monthly payments, but the new mortgage will have to be paid off over a longer period of time. In addition, there are generally refinance charges that must be paid.

A HOME MORTGAGE IS REFINANCED WHEN THE ORIGINAL LOAN IS PAID OFF BEFORE IT MATURES AND A NEW LOAN IS TAKEN OUT ON THE SAME PROPERTY. HOME MORTGAGE REFINANCING ALSO REFERS TO TAKING OUT A SECOND MORTGAGE BASED ON THE EQUITY IN THE HOUSE.

To understand the way in which a refinancing decision should be made, consider the three illustrations given in Exhibit 10. In case A the family has an old mortgage of 17 percent that it has been paying for 10 years. The monthly payment is $1,425. In case B the family has an old mortgage of 12 percent that it has been paying for 10 years, with a monthly payment of $1,029. In case C the family has an old mortgage of 10 percent that it has been paying for 15 years, with a monthly payment of $878.

Exhibit 10
Case Illustrations of Refinancing of Mortgage

Items in the Mortgage	Case A	Case B	Case C
Total loan amount	$100,000	$100,000	$100,000
Interest rate	17%	12%	10%
Years of loan	30	30	30
Monthly payment	$1,427	$1,029	$878
Years paid on loan	10	10	15
Balance of principal	$96,994	$92,708	$80,285
New interest rate	8%	8%	8%
New monthly payment	$707	$676	$585
Difference in monthly payment	$718	$353	$293
Refinance charge (5%)	$4,849	$4,635	$4,014
Total old payout	$342,000	$246,960	$158,040
Total new payout	$259,362	$247,995	$214,614
Difference in payouts (old payout – new payout)	+$82,638	–$1,035	–$56,574

SOURCE: Calculation by author

The family in case A, which has the opportunity to get a 9 percentage point reduction in its interest and can save $718 in monthly payments, is clearly better off by refinancing. The family can afford to pay a mortgage for the longer period under the new mortgage.

The family in case B will realize a 4 percentage point reduction in its interest rate, with a reduction of its monthly payment of $676. However, it will actually pay out more by refinancing. Although the new payout will come from cheaper dollars, the value to the family may make refinancing questionable under these circumstances. If the refinance charges are higher than the 5 percent shown in the exhibit, that alone can wipe out the advantages gained from the refinancing.

The family in case C clearly should not refinance its mortgage. Although it will reduce its monthly payment by $293, that will be wiped out by the refinance charges and the much larger interest payments that the family will have to make. Once the family has paid on a mortgage for 15 years, it is rarely possible to be better off by refinancing, even when the interest rate is much lower. This is because of the high interest payments that would start all over again and the new 30-year mortgage, instead of the 15 years remaining on the old mortgage.

The decision to refinance will depend on the costs of refinancing compared to the costs of continuing with the current loan. For example, there are costs associated with refinancing and the terms of the loan that may make the existing loan more attractive even though the interest rate is higher. Some of the factors that will determine whether to refinance include:

- The length of time the family expects to remain at the current residence. If you expect to move within five years, it may not make a lot of sense to refinance. This would need to be calculated carefully.
- The difference between the interest rate on the current mortgage and the best interest rate the family can get under refinancing. If the interest rate difference is less than 3 percent, it probably doesn't make a lot of sense to refinance.
- The amount of time remaining on the loan. If the payment toward principal exceeds the payment toward interest, it probably doesn't make a lot of sense to refinance.
- The overall financial standing of the family.
- Changes in the family composition since the original loan was taken out.

When in doubt about whether it is financially prudent for your family to refinance its mortgage, check with an independent bank or mortgage company and ask for a detailed assessment of the advantages and disadvantages of refinancing.

IF YOU ARE GOING TO REFINANCE YOUR HOUSE WITH A NEW MORTGAGE, TAKE OUT A 15-YEAR MORTGAGE INSTEAD OF A NEW 30-YEAR MORTGAGE.

Should you refinance to purchase items or pay for college?—It is important to realize that refinancing permits you to take out some of the equity in your home without selling your house. This type of refinancing is usually through a *second mortgage*.

A SECOND MORTGAGE IS A LOAN ON THE EQUITY VALUE OF YOUR HOUSE. EQUITY VALUE IS THE DIFFERENCE BETWEEN THE MARKET VALUE OF YOUR HOUSE AND THE REMAINING PRINCIPAL BALANCE ON THE MORTGAGE.

A second mortgage can be useful under certain conditions, and a financial disaster under other conditions. Many mortgage companies and banks are offering a *"home-equity line of credit."*

These lines of credit are attractive to many families because they offer easy money. Once you have a line of credit, it is possible to take out new money up to your credit line. These funds can be used for any purpose you choose, but only part of the interest payments will be tax-deductible.

There are several things that the family should remember about a second mortgage line of credit that should make it pause before going down that path.

- The second mortgage will usually take a collateralized loan, with the house as collateral, and substitute for a noncollateralized loan, such as credit card bills. The risk has then been transferred to the house.
- The second mortgage uses your house as collateral. If for some reason you should not be able to pay the second mortgage, you could lose your house.
- In a second mortgage, usually for 15 years, you will make payment for debts that generally require only a few years to pay off. The interest payments can be enormous.
- With a second mortgage, getting out of debt will take much longer. Even when the interest payments are at lower rates than credit cards, you may be better off paying the higher rates for a short time than a low rate for a long time.
- A second mortgage line of credit reduces the amount of equity in your house by the amount of credit used and all fees associated with establishing the second mortgage.

The bottom line is this: The Christian family should avoid a second mortgage under most circumstances, if possible. If funds are needed to pay for college education for the children, consider taking out a direct loan. Consolidation loans are usually a bad deal. Consider this: Would you like to pay for a credit card bill for the next 15 years? That is likely what you will do if you take out a consolidation loan.

Under the right circumstances, the second mortgage can be a means of dealing with a drastic financial condition. In the absence of such conditions, *avoid a second mortgage or a second mortgage line of credit.*

Summary

A house is a store of wealth for most families and represents their most valuable financial resource. Renting is not as financially profitable, but it may be the only option available to the family.

If the family has the ability to buy, then the decision to continue to rent or to buy a house is one of the more important financing decisions to be made. It should be made prayerfully and with as much information as the family is able to obtain. That information includes being able to compare the financial implications of one alternative against another. In addition, the family should be familiar with the common themes and ideas that are part of the costs and benefits of housing.

Always take a look at the financial advantages associated with alternative financing approaches and the number of years of financing the house. Settle on the financing method that offers the family the best financial advantages and leaves the family best off. Go over all the numbers carefully and consider the costs.

6

Buying and Leasing a Car

Few things fascinate individuals as much as cars, the modern chariots. Cars represent more than just transportation. For many, cars help define their personalities, show off their wealth and good taste, and demonstrate their passion for power. Cars are pampered, and probably the average person spends more time in the car each week than at church. When Christians spend too much money on cars, spend too much time with them, or use them to exalt self, then the car becomes an idol.

How Much Will We Spend on Cars?

Throughout a lifetime the average family will spend more on a car than on college education and on any single purchase except housing. The cost of shelter is usually the single most expensive purchase in any family's budget; buying a car is frequently the second most expensive. Between the ages of 20 and 65 the average individual will buy 10 to 15 cars and will spend the equivalent of $12,000 each in 1993 dollars for them. With the interest charges on the financing of cars, with maintenance and upkeep costs, the individual can easily spend $200,000 to $300,000 in a lifetime on automobile costs. If the family buys more expensive cars, this figure can go up substantially.

How Many Cars Does the Family Need?

Depending on where the family lives and its access to public transportation, they usually regard a car as a necessity, not a luxury. Even when public transportation is readily available, owning (or leasing) a car is a major convenience.

When there are two working adults in the family, the family must determine whether more than one car is needed. In the past a two-car family was pretty much a rarity, but now it is becoming less so as more women work outside the home and must have an independent means of transportation. In some families it is not unusual to find teenagers also owning cars. Thus, whether a family owns one or more cars will depend on the needs of the workers in the household, the distance that each worker has to go to reach work, the availability of public transportation, and the financial circumstances of the family.

Why Do People Buy Different Kinds of Cars?

A car means different things to different people. Its basic function is, of course, to be a means of transportation. That transportation must be safe, and it must be reliable. We must feel that the car has been designed in such a way that if there is an accident, it will provide as much safety as possible. Most new car buyers want the current safety features, including an air bag and an antilock braking system (ABS). We also want to feel certain that the car will start and give us reliable service when we need to use it.

People buy cars for a large number of reasons.

- A car says something about the tastes of its owner.
- A car is selected for its apparent style.
- A car is chosen for its power and ability to go fast.
- A car is selected to impress the observer.
- A car is a status symbol to show off the owner's wealth.

For the 1993 car year a new car cost as little as $8,000 and as much as $130,000! Most new cars, however, cost between $12,000 and $30,000. Cars costing more than $30,000 are considered luxury cars.

Can the Christian Family Justify Buying a Luxury Car?

ON FINANCIAL, SAFETY, AND COMFORT GROUNDS, IT IS VERY DIFFICULT FOR THE AVERAGE FAMILY TO JUSTIFY PURCHASING A CAR COSTING MORE THAN $30,000.

Justification for purchasing a luxury car is made on the basis of safety, riding comfort, and durability of the product. However, the two most important safety features—air bags and antilock brakes—are available on cars costing far less than $30,000. Some of these cars also have better safety records than do cars costing tens of thousands more. Riding comfort is very subjective, but it can be obtained from cars costing much less than luxury cars.

Who, then, purchases these luxury cars? Persons who can easily afford such cars, and all too many who really cannot afford them. When families who cannot afford such luxuries purchase expensive cars in an effort to show off their wealth, they are acting in a financially irresponsible—and morally questionable—manner.

How Much Should the Family Pay for Any One Car?

There are three basic options when the family needs a car:

- Buy a new car.
- Lease a new car.
- Buy a used car.

Each option presents various trade-offs between costs and convenience that the family will have to decide. For some families, a new car is desirable because it is likely to be more trouble-free and reliable. For other families, the lower price of a used car fits better into the family's budget. For still others, leasing a car (which is essentially a long-term rental agreement) permits conservation of capital and the enjoyment of a new car's benefits.

Costs of buying a new car.—A new car provides reliability and a certain thrill. However, a car is a wasting asset—that is, its value is steadily eroding. Immediately after buying a new car, the resale value falls dramatically. Within one year and 15,000 miles a new car can easily lose 20 to 30 percent of its purchase value. Buying a new car requires a large outlay of money for several years. Consider what the down payment and monthly payment would be for cars that range in negotiated price from $10,000 to $25,000, as shown in Table 12. (These costs assume a 10 percent annual interest rate and a down payment that is 20 percent of the total cost.) Note that the family can finance for three, four, or five years. As the payment period increases, the monthly payment decreases.

Longer payment periods mean more payment of interest. As Table 12 shows, the monthly payments can range upward of $684 per month for luxury cars that are financed for a short period. In addition to the car payments, the costs of maintenance and repair, tires, gasoline, oil, insurance, parking fees, taxes, and depreciation may average between 20 cents and 35 cents per mile, depending on the type of car. (By way of comparison, the federal government allows 26 cents per mile to be claimed if individuals use a personal car while conducting government business.)

Table 12
Cost Involved in Buying a New Car

Negotiated Price	$10,000	$15,000	$17,500	$20,000	$25,000
Taxes (6%)	600	900	1,050	1,200	1,500
Total Cost	$10,600	$15,900	$18,550	$21,200	$26,500
Down Payment (20%)	2,120	3,180	3,710	4,240	5,300
Amount Financed	$8,480	$12,720	$14,840	$16,960	$21,200
Monthly Payments (10% Annual Interest Rate)					
3 years	$273.63	$410.44	$478.85	$547.25	$684.06
4 years	215.07	322.61	376.38	430.15	537.69
5 years	180.17	270.26	315.31	360.35	450.44
Total Payments					
3 years	$11,971	$17,956	$20,948	$23,941	$29,926
4 years	12,444	18,665	21,776	24,887	31,109
5 years	12,930	19,396	22,628	25,861	32,326

NOTE: By adding up any two columns you can get the results for higher priced cars. For example, to find the costs associated with a $35,000 car, add the columns for the $10,000 and the $25,000 cars.

Table 13 provides an illustration of what a car may cost per month. This table shows that if the family owns a car with a high cost of operation, its cost can range up to $291.67 per month when 10,000 miles per year are driven, and a whopping $875.00 a month when the car is driven 30,000 miles. When operating expenses are added to the monthly car payments, it is clear that car ownership is a very expensive undertaking.

Table 13
Estimated Monthly Costs of Operating a Car

Miles Driven Per Year	Average Cost Per Mile		
	$0.20	$0.30	$0.35
	Costs Per Month		
10,000 miles	$166.67	$250.00	$291.67
15,000 miles	250,00	375.00	437.50
20,000 miles	333.33	500.00	583.33
30,000 miles	500.00	750.00	875.00

Should the Family Buy a New or Used Car?

Cars serve the basic function of providing transportation. In this society it also satisfies an additional need. For many individuals a car is a statement about who they are and what their status in life is. When carried to its extreme, a car becomes an extension of the individual and proclaims to the world that person's self-image. Some analysts have suggested that the type of car, the color, and the size have a lot to say about the mental position of the individual.

If Christians are to be modest in their outward adornment, how much more should they show modesty in their choice of cars? It is not always obvious whether it is more prudent to fix up the old but still useful car one more time or to purchase a new car.

Perhaps the most critical factor should be whether or not the old car can provide safe, reliable transportation. If breakdowns occur randomly and without warning, the family could be greatly inconvenienced or even placed in danger. If an older car has random breakdowns that start to cause workers to be late to or miss important functions, then it may be time to buy a new car. Of course, well-maintained used cars offer a reasonable alternative when the family cannot afford a new car.

The important principle to remember is that a car's major function is to provide transportation. When a car is used to express ostentation or to show off the family's affluence, then the Christian family should beware. And under no circumstances should the family become burdened with the purchase of a car that is beyond their means. The danger then is that giving to the Lord's work could be sacrificed in order to enjoy the pleasures of a new car.

What About Leasing a Car?

A car lease may be the preferred way to obtain use of a car. The major features of a car lease are as follows:

Positive aspects of leasing:

- A leased car requires a smaller down payment. Leasing allows you to lower your monthly outlay of cash.
- Leasing allows you to change cars more frequently without using up your cash.
- Virtually any car can be leased.

Not so positive aspects of leasing:

- You will not own the car unless you buy it after the lease.
- Most leases charge for excess mileage (usually more than 15,000 miles a year).
- You will pay for any damage to the car above simple wear and tear.

You can benefit from leasing if you don't drive many miles a year and if you change cars frequently. Otherwise, leasing may not be for you. To illustrate the differences, take a look at Table 14, which compares the advantages of buying a new car, a used car, and leasing. Of course, your individual tastes will help you decide what is best for you.

Table 14
Comparison of the Costs of Buying Versus Leasing

	Car A		Car B		Car C	
Sale Price	$17,100		$18,490		$29,990	
	Buy	Lease	Buy	Lease	Buy	Lease
Down Payment	$3,700	$1,200	$3,500	$3,500	$3,500	$3,500
No. of Months	60	24	48	36	60	36
Monthly Payments	$299	$299	$394	$239	$589	$395
Total Payments	$17,940	$7,176	$18,912	$8,604	$35,340	$14,220
Total Outlays = Payments + Down Payment	$21,640	$8,376	$22,412	$12,104	$38,840	$17,720
Residual to Purchase	—	$13,313	—	$10,573	—	$19,636
Mileage Limitation	None	15,000	None	15,000	None	15,000
Charge for Excess Miles	None	$.15/m	None	$.15/m	None	$.15/m

SOURCE: Local newspaper advertisement of actual cars for sale and lease.

7

College Education: Its Rewards and Cost

One of the joys and obligations of Christian parents is to encourage their children to prepare themselves for a life work. To an increasing extent this means that the children's education must include college. But college can be very expensive. As a result, parents need to engage in systematic financial preparation. This chapter explores the rewards and cost of college training. It presents the Christian family several alternative models for selecting an appropriate college and modes for its finance.

Is College Training Worth the Cost?

It should first be observed that college training is both an investment and a consumption. The parents, and increasingly the children, invest in the education for the benefits it will provide for future employment. Education is also a consumption good. The college experience permits exploration of the beauties of nature. In a Christian setting, college permits deeper study about the God of the universe. The theme of salvation may be more fully examined under the careful tutelage of dedicated teachers.

AFTER ADJUSTING FOR RACE AND SEX, UNDER AVERAGE CONDITIONS THE HIGHER THE LEVEL OF EDUCATION THE GREATER THE EARNINGS.

The college experience also permits children to delve into topics that stimulate the mind—mathematics, science, poetry, languages, social studies, art, business. Students are encouraged to expand God's great gift of a curious mind. While exploration goes on outside the classroom, it is in the college setting that these factors are most focused. For the young and not-so-young, the college setting provides a marvelous opportunity for mental, social, spiritual, and emotional growth.

College graduates earn more.—College graduates, on average, earn more money throughout their lifetime than those of similar characteristics who do not graduate from college. It is important to note that the returns on the investment in college education will vary with the race and sex of the person. This is shown very clearly in Table 15, which compares the average annual wage and salary income of individuals who finish various levels of education.

Table 15
Comparison of Returns to Education

	HIGHEST LEVEL OF EDUCATION					
	8 Years or Less	9-12 Years (no H.S. diploma)	H.S. Diploma	1-4 Years of College (no B.A. degree)	College Graduate (B.A. degree)	Graduate Degree (M.A. level)
Males						
White	20,003	24,425	29,736	35,230	47,080	54,371
Black	19,737	20,020	22,803	28,494	33,581	46,234
Females						
White	13,777	15,831	20,271	23,778	31,605	37,391
Black	13,157	13,310	18,629	21,488	29,940	34,474

SOURCE: U. S. Bureau of the Census, *Money Income of Households, Families, and Persons in the United States: 1992,* Table 29, Consumer Income Series P60-184. Washington, D.C., 1993.

NOTE: These are annual average earnings of full-time, year-round workers.

We see, for example, that among whites a person who completes only the eighth grade will, on average, earn $20,000 per year if male, but only $13,777, if female. A high school graduate will earn, on average, $29,736 or $20,271; a college graduate will earn, on average, $47,080 or $31,605; those possessing a graduate degree will earn $54,371 or $37,391, for males and females, respectively.

Table 15 also shows that Whites, on average, earn more than Blacks, and that men earn more than women. Studies on the return of investments in education have consistently shown that once race and sex are accounted for, education pays. Thus, while it is true that Black males who graduate from college, for example, earn less than White males who do not finish college, they earn more than Black males who do not attend or complete college. Women who complete college earn more than their sisters who do not attend or complete, although, on average, they earn less than males who do not attend college.

For the Christian family, earnings are not the only reason for attending college. Those who do attend, however, are rewarded by higher earnings and the opportunity for a professional career.

College Costs Can Vary Widely

There are more than 1,350 four-year colleges and 1,200 two-year community colleges in the United States. The costs of tuition, room, and board for these colleges range from nominal fees that are less than $3,000 a year to costs of more than $25,000 a year at the most prestigious colleges and universities.

Numerous factors account for the varying costs of a college education. These include the type of school (public versus private), whether the public college is in the state of the student's residence, whether the student lives in a dormitory or at home, and whether a four-year college is chosen rather than a two-year community college. Everything else being equal, the factors divide along the lines shown in Exhibit 11.

Exhibit 11

Factors That Cause Higher Costs	Factors That Cause Lower Costs
Private College	Public College
Public Out-of-State	Public In-State
Live in Dormitory	Live at Home
Four-year College	Two-Year Community College

Thus if the Christian family chooses a private college, then it can save by having the student reside at home. If a public college is chosen, then, in general, tuition charges are greater to the student who is not a resident of the state than they are for students who are residents.

These are greatly simplifying factors and may not be applicable for the particular situation of a given family. A family may wish the child to attend a Christian college. Many such colleges are located in small towns and require that the student live in the college dormitory.

Cost estimates of various colleges.—The ideal way for the Christian family to choose a college for the children is to select the college according to the Christian ideals that the parents want imparted and be concerned about the costs later on. However, this is not always practical.

To an increasing extent the students themselves determine the type of college they want to attend. The availability of scholarship money can often play a role in the selection, as can such things as proximity to home and the specialties of the school. The value of the spiritual, cultural, social, and physical attributes of the school also play a role.

The major categories of expenses for college are:

- tuition
- room and board
- books and fees
- miscellaneous living and travel expenses

Financial planning for these expenses must include an inflation factor for the number of years before the student starts school and the rate of increase in expenses once school starts.

Table 16 shows how tuition, room, and board can vary across selected colleges and universities. At the most prestigious research-oriented universities the average tuition is about $14,000 per year. Another $5,000 will go for room and board. These rates are for the 1990-1991 school year. The average tuition at selected Christian colleges was $7,748. Room and board added another $3,049, making a total of $10,797. In addition to these costs, there are the books, fees, and the occasional trip back home. These miscellaneous costs can easily add $1,000 to the annual costs.

The costs shown in Table 16 must be adjusted for future inflationary growth. By the time your children attend college, the cost will be much higher!

Table 17 shows the adjustment factor that you must use to get some idea of future college costs for your children. From the table, select the type of college you want your child to attend. Find the adjustment factor by estimating how many years it will be before your children enter college. Then multiply that factor by the one-year and four-year estimates. This is an approximation of what tuition, room, and board will cost you by the time your children go to college. To this must be added the costs of books, fees, transportation, and miscellaneous expenses. Such costs can easily add $2,000 to $3,000 to the annual college expense.

Table 16
Estimates of One-Year and Four-Year Costs at Selected Colleges

College Type	Tuition	Room and Board	First Year Total	Four-Year Total
Prestigious, Top 25 University	$14,367	$5,241	$19,608	$85,777
Four-Year State College				
State Resident	1,493	2,752	4,245	18,570
Out-of-State	3,740	2,752	6,492	28,400
Four-Year State University				
State Resident	1,952	3,617	5,569	24,362
Out-of-State	5,358	3,617	8,975	39,262
Small, Private Liberal Arts College	9,003	3,835	12,838	56,161
Adventist College	7,748	3,049	10,797	47,233

NOTES: These estimates represent 22 colleges and universities selected from states in which there are Seventh-day Adventist colleges, and from information on the top 25 universities in the country. One public state college, the principal university of the state, and one representative private, nonsectarian, liberal arts college were selected from each such state. The data on tuition and room and board for the selected colleges come from *U.S. News and World Report's* "America's Best Colleges," 1991 edition. The costs were inflated at the rate of 6% per year.

An illustration will show what it will cost to send a child who is 8 years old in 1992 to an Adventist college in the year 2002. Using the assumption of 6 percent college cost inflation, the estimated cost will be about $84,800 for the four years. It should be noted that during that time average wages and salaries will be rising by about 4.5 percent per year.

These numbers seem terribly high. What is the Christian family to do?

Table 17
Conversion Chart for Estimating Future College Needs

Years to Start College	Adjustment Factor	Years to Start College	Adjustment Factor
1	1.06	10	1.79
2	1.12	11	1.89
3	1.19	12	2.01
4	1.26	13	2.13
5	1.34	14	2.26
6	1.42	15	2.39
7	1.51	16	2.54
8	1.59	17	2.69
9	1.69	18	2.85

NOTE: This chart provides for the compounding at 6% of the rate of future college costs. The actual inflation rate may be greater or smaller.

How Is College Education Financed?

Very few parents pay cash for all the expenses of their children's college education. College students often receive scholarships based on academics, athletics, or hardship. Grants and loans are available, depending on the family's income and expenses. In addition, the student may work to supplement other forms of college finance. In short, there are numerous ways and combinations to finance college education for the Christian family.

Gifts.—Parents are the major source of gifts to finance education. The amount of the parents' gifts will depend on the parents' ability and willingness. Other gifts can come from a variety of sources, including friends, church groups, and others interested in the education of the young. In some instances, gifts will come from strangers who provide special funds for needy students.

If a student is applying for financial assistance, the school will require parental assistance based on family income and assets. However, not all parents can afford to give according to the school's schedule. There may be other children and expense needs. This is especially true when the parents support other children in church schools or when more than one child is in college at a time. There may be only one parent in the home, and that parent may not have sufficient income to support a child's college education.

The parent(s) can finance their children's education by:

- using current income on a pay-as-you-go system.
- saving for college during the child's early years.
- borrowing against the equity in the home or against future income.

Scholarships.—Scholarships are forms of financial assistance usually given on condition to students who fit into special categories. The student may be eligible for a wide array of scholarships, ranging from academic, athletic, special category, or need-based. The scholarships may be given to students to take to the school of their choice, or they may be given on condition of attending a particular school. Scholarships may pay for part of the costs of one year or several years. Some scholarships will pay the full cost of tuition, room, and board.

Colleges and universities may issue scholarships on the basis of the special characteristics of the student, such as ethnic-, racial-, or gender-based designations. Many colleges and universities will almost always make scholarships available to students who score very high (score of 1,200 or more out of 1,600 total points) on the Scholastic Aptitude Test (SAT). Scholarships are sometimes offered to satisfy schools' needs to diversify their student body.

States may offer scholarships to students who are residents of the state and who go to a public or private institution within the state. In some instances, state scholarships are available for students to take with them to a school in another state.

Scholarships will vary with the level of college attained. In general, scholarship funds are more available to the graduate student than to the undergraduate, and to upper-level undergraduates than to lower division students.

The more flexible students are with regard to where they will go to school or the type of school they will attend, the greater the number of scholarships available. However, the Christian family may want to choose carefully the college to which they send their children. This will mean that some scholarships will not be available or attractive to them.

Loans.—For many families, loans are a significant part of the financing of the child's college education. Funds may be lent to the family to provide as gifts to the child, or the loans may be made to the college student, who will pay them back after the college education is completed. There are many forms of loans available to the Christian family.

Stafford loans, formerly called Guaranteed Student loans, are issued by a bank and are provided to any student enrolled in an accepted college or vocational training program. The maximum amount of the loan is $4,000 per year, depending on the college cost. Interest is set at 8 percent, and the student does not have to begin repayment until after the college education is completed or the student no longer attends college.

The federal government pays the accrued interest, guarantees the loan to the bank that issues it, pays the bank a premium to make sure the bank receives a market rate of return, and assumes the loan if the student defaults.

Students may apply for a Stafford loan directly from a local bank once a college has been selected. The bank will determine the eligibility of the student and the institution, and process the loan. Students, not their parent(s), will be responsible to repay the loan.

Perkins loans are campus-based loans that the college or university applies for directly from the Department of Education. The school then lends the money to students, based on the formula set by the program and the school to determine need. Perkins loans are part of a revolving fund in which students pay back the money lent out by the school so that future students will have a chance to borrow.

Students may borrow up to $4,500 per school year. Repayment is deferred until the student graduates or no longer attends college. The interest rates are lower than commercial rates but are slightly higher than Stafford loan interest rates.

Students can apply for Perkins loans directly from the college they plan to attend. The student, not the parent(s), is responsible for the repayment of the loan. The college is guaranteed access to additional future funds in the event of default. However, if a significant percentage of students from a given institution defaults on the loan, the ability of the college to lend funds to future students can be jeopardized.

Parents can always go into the commercial market to borrow money to finance the education of their children. They can borrow against the equity in their home (a second mortgage) or against their anticipated future income. The ability to borrow will depend on their credit rating, their income, and the extent of their debts.

The federal government provides loans to parents through the *Parent Loans for Undergraduate Students* (PLUS). Loans of up to $4,000 are made to parents, who are then responsible for their repayment. Loan repayment begins immediately, rather than being deferred, as in the case of the Stafford and Perkins loans programs.

The important things to remember about loans include:

- There should be a clear understanding between parent(s) and student about how much will be borrowed for each year.
- The terms of the loan should be clearly understood. The student should know clearly what the interest rate is, when the loan is to be repaid, and how much will have to be paid out each month.
- It should be made clear that the Christian student has a moral obligation to repay an honest debt, even when it is painful.

Grants.—Grants are direct gifts to help finance college education. These grants may be made by federal, state, or local governments, or by the school itself. Grants come in all forms and sizes, and in some respects may look like scholarships. One distinguishing characteristic is that federal grants are usually need-based.

Students from families whose incomes fall below a target amount may qualify for special need-based grants. The popularly named *Pell grants* are provided to students in the amounts of $200 to $2,200 per year. The amount of the grant will depend on need (as defined by family income and debt), the cost of the college attended, the length of the college program, and whether the student is a full-time or part-time student.

The amount of funding for Pell grants has fallen in recent years, and these grants are generally limited to families with the lowest incomes.

Another type of grant designed to assist families with low adjusted incomes or who already receive financial assistance is the *Special Economic Opportunity Grants* (SEOG). Unlike Pell grants, which are given to the student by the federal government, SEOG grants are campus-based. Funds are provided to the school, and the school makes grants directly to the student. Maximum grants are up to $4,000 per year. These funds tend to be limited and are highly competed for.

Work-Study Programs.—Many college programs started out with the goal of assisting the development of the head, heart, soul, and hand. Work-study programs were started with the schools of the prophets during the time of Elijah and Elisha. The development of manual skills while the mind is also being developed is in the greatest tradition of Christian education.

Current work-study programs are far more limited than even a generation ago. Few students are able to support their education through their work earnings alone. Instead many students take part-time work during the school year and full-time work during the summers to help finance their education.

Conclusions

There are many ways to finance college education. Few students have their education financed solely through gifts from their parents. Few receive scholarships that pay for the entire costs. Instead most students use a combination of gifts, grants, scholarships, loans, and work.

8

Borrowing and Debt

One of the most misunderstood aspects of financial planning is that associated with borrowing and debt. Today few Christian families can avoid debt. It has frequently been recognized as a moral hazard and one that should be avoided. However, few families know how. Fewer still are the families that understand how Christians can plan for debt management. These and other issues are the focus of this chapter.

What Is Debt?

Debt is money, services, or materials owed to someone else. Debt arises from a specific contractual arrangement or agreement between two parties. There are several advantages of debt that make it attractive to many families.

- Debt permits purchase of necessary items that would not be affordable as a cash purchase.
- Debt reduces the need to carry large amounts of cash.
- Debt is the only way to make purchases for some goods and services (billed services, like telephone or medical).
- Debt permits the family to enhance the quality of life.
- Debt permits emergency purchases like travel.

How Much Debt Should the Christian Family Have?

The amount of debt that the Christian family should have will depend on the type of debt, the total amount of assets, and the amount of income that the family has to support debt. Families that are buying houses will likely have a different debt structure from families that are renting. Also, families with high incomes will likely have a very different debt structure from families with low incomes.

How to Know When Debt Is Excessive

The Christian family will know that their debt is excessive when:

- they are unable to return a faithful tithe because of the press of bills.
- there is not enough money left over, after bills are paid, to put into savings.
- there is a systematic juggling of bills so that some are paid in one month while others are deferred until the next month.
- money has to be borrowed to meet the expenses of daily necessities, such as food and transportation.
- bills are consistently past due, and legal action has been started by creditors seeking payment.
- the family is more concerned about its finances than its spiritual condition.

When these things happen, the family and its members may be in serious spiritual and financial condition. Long before this situation occurs the Christian family must understand the proper use of the credit that leads to debt. But if this situation is present, the Christian family must take immediate steps to get out of debt.

First, let us examine some of the basic concepts of what constitutes good debt management.

How much interest should you pay?—Debt almost always requires the payment of interest. Normally, debt that lasts for more than 30 days will require the payment of interest. Interest charges increase the cost of whatever is provided on credit. The interest rate charged will depend on:

- the amount of the debt.
- whether the debt is secured by collateral.
- the amount of the down payment made by the purchaser.
- the nature of the debt.
- the creditworthiness of the individual.
- the particular lender.

The interest rate is stated as an annual percentage amount and will vary with the economic conditions in the country. For example, in 1993 home mortgage interest rates ranged from 6 percent to 10 percent, depending on the terms. Automobile loan interest rates ranged from 8 percent to 12 percent, depending on whether the car was new or used, the amount of the down payment, and the length of the loan. Consumer cash loans may range from 12 percent to 30 percent, depending on the amount of the loan, the loan period, and the type of lender.

The annual percentage amount will vary, depending on how often the interest is compounded. If the interest rate is stated as 8 percent and if the interest is *compounded daily*, the annual percentage rate (APR) is actually 8.33 percent. The important things for the Christian family to remember when going into debt are:

- shop around for the lowest interest rate.
- know exactly what interest rates are being paid.
- keep a record of how much interest is being paid as a means of comparing future expenditures.

Interest rates for consumer purchases are no longer deductible from income in determining income taxes. However, interest payments are still a reduction from your disposable income. Therefore, try to keep interest payments as low as possible.

The length of the debt period affects the interest paid.—The longer the debt period, the smaller the amount of the monthly payback. However, when the payment period is extended, greater interest payments are incurred, since the family is using someone else's money for a longer period.

How Much Does Consumer Credit Really Cost?

How much does credit really cost? The data in Table 18 show what interest you could end up paying for the privilege of buying on credit. If a family goes $1,000 into debt and pays off the debt in monthly installments during one year, the total interest payment at 8 percent (8.33 percent APR) is $83. However, if the debt is extended to three years, the total interest payments go all the way up to $270; after five years the interest payments are $490.

Consider the typical payment for credit cards at 21 percent annual interest. If you make payments on $1,000 of debt during one year, you will pay $231 in interest. If you pay off this debt by the end of five years, you will pay a whopping $1,832 in interest charges in addition to the repayment of the original $1,000. Now, it should be noted that these payments are made with cheaper dollars and that few creditors will allow for five years of payments. But the potential for high interest payments is greater than you may imagine.

Although the monthly payments are smaller when the payment period is longer, the total interest payments are much larger. Many charge accounts, such as those provided by department stores and credit cards like Visa and MasterCard, charge between 18 and 21 percent and let you pay in small installments. Lenders are usually content to let you make small payments, because it means that interest payments are locked in for a longer period of time.

Table 18
Total Interest Payments by Years and Rates for Every $1,000 in Debt

	Annual Interest Rate			
	8%	12%	18%	21%
Years	Total Interest Payments			
1	$ 83	$127	$ 196	$ 231
3	270	431	709	867
5	490	817	1,443	1,832

Determining How Much Debt You Want to Have

The debt-asset ratio.—The debt-asset ratio is the ratio of total debts to the appropriate value of the assets. For example, if you buy a house for $100,000 and pay $20,000 down, you will have a debt of $80,000. Your debt-asset ratio will be $80,000/$100,000, or 80 percent. However, if you pay only $5,000 down, your debt-asset ratio will be 95 percent. If your debts exceed your assets, your debt-asset ratio is larger than 100 percent, and you are technically insolvent.

If you sum all assets, give them a current market value, and then calculate their debt, that is your debt-asset ratio. Realistically speaking, only houses and cars tend to have an established market value. Dear as your electronic equipment and furniture are, it is not likely that you will know what their value is. Use Table 19 to calculate your debt-asset ratio.

The debt flow-income flow ratio.—Another way of looking at debt is by the amount of debt service (your bills) compared to the amount of income. This is the debt flow-income flow ratio. For example, if you sum all debt items in your budget (not including daily living expenses and such) and divide that by the amount of regular income, you have the debt flow-income flow ratio.

THE LOWER THE DEBT-ASSET RATIO, THE BETTER THE DEBT POSITION.

Table 19
Calculation of the Debt-Asset Ratio

Item	Cost at Purchase	Current Value	Current Amount of Debt
REAL ESTATE			
House you occupy			
House rented out 1			
House rent out 2			
AUTOMOBILES			
Car 1			
Car 2			
Car 3			
ELECTRONICS			
Value of all TVs			
Value of all cameras			
Value of all other electronics			
FURNITURE			
ALL OTHER MARKETABLE ITEMS			
TOTALS			
CURRENT DEBT/ CURRENT VALUE			

WHEN THE DEBT-ASSET RATION EXCEEDS 90 PERCENT; OR WHEN DEBT FLOW, NOT COUNTING HOUSING COSTS, EXCEEDS *35 PERCENT* OF AFTER-TAX INCOME, THE FAMILY IS IN DANGER OF FINANCIAL DISTRESS.

Not All Debt Is Bad!

Although some debt is unavoidable, there are three questions that should be asked before any debt is incurred.

	YES	NO
1. Can this new debt be avoided without disrupting the smooth function of the family?	❑	❑
2. Can this debt be avoided by some judicious short-term savings?	❑	❑
3. Will this debt severely strain the family's financial resources?	❑	❑

Unless the answer is no to all three questions, the Christian family should be very careful about entering into debt, regardless of the purpose.

Not all debt that a family has or incurs is bad. Debt is sometimes necessary in order for the family to leverage their income into the purchase of goods and services that would not otherwise be available. Debt may be used to pay for: (1) capital goods, (2) transitory goods, and (3) services. Some examples are given in Exhibit 12.

Exhibit 12
Three Types of Debt

Capital Goods		Transitory Goods		Billed Services	
Item	Debt?	Item	Debt?	Item	Debt?
Houses	Y	Clothing	N	Utility bills	N
Automobiles	Y	Restaurant meals	N	Medical bills	Y
Major Appliances	Y	Gasoline	N	Legal fees	Y
Furniture	Y	Small appliances	N	Household services	Y

Kinds of Debt

Debt for capital goods.—Few families are willing to save until they are able to pay cash for major purchases. Indeed, because of inflation, the prices for all goods and services are steadily increasing. To pay cash would require that the family set aside large amounts of its current income. For many purchases, paying cash is practical only for the affluent. Thus, families incur debt to obtain those items that it would be too difficult to save for.

Debt for transitory goods.—Under most conditions, transitory goods should not be purchased through debt. Goods and services consumed on a regular basis—items like clothing, food, gasoline, and small appliances—often are purchased with credit cards. Since these items are usually purchased in amounts that are relatively inexpensive, the use of debt is viewed as a convenience. Yet it is frequently with purchases such as these that the Christian family can find itself deeply in debt and in financial distress.

Debt for billed services.—Debt may arise because of billed services—the normal monthly bills for such things as telephone service and utilities. Billed services may also include special purpose billing such as for medical or legal sources and for infrequent household maintenance items. In most such instances there are no interest costs or carrying charges if payments are made within 30 days. In these instances, debt is unavoidable. However, to the extent possible, the family should choose to pay by check immediately upon receipt of a bill. If allowed to grow, these billed services can become major debts.

Debt from borrowing cash.—Debt may also take the form of borrowed cash. This can be done through a line of credit at the bank, a personal or signature loan through the credit union or a finance company, or through the refinancing of a home. Unlike debt for goods or services, this type of debt places cash directly into the hands of the family.

Cash is often borrowed for such things as a vacation, for speculative purposes, for home improvements, or other desires. While these items may be greatly needed, cash can pass through the hands very quickly. In a relatively short period, this cash can be gone, but the debt will remain. For many Christian families it is the *most dangerous* form of debt.

The Many Dangers of Debt

There are many dangers associated with debt, especially debt that consumes too much of the Christian family's income. Debt may:

- provide a false sense of financial well-being.
- permit the easy indulgence in goods and services that are not necessary for a full life.
- interfere with our obligations to God and with Christian service.

- become the source of family distress.

To understand these advantages and disadvantages more clearly, it is useful to examine God's plan for us as stewards. We begin with the notion that *all* we have belongs to the Lord and that what we have has been lent to us. Next, the admonition is given: "The wicked borrow and do not repay, but the righteous give generously" (Ps. 37:21).

Ten principles on debt from the writings of Ellen White may help us understand the role of debt. These are presented in Exhibit 13.

Exhibit 13
Ten Principles on Debt From the Spirit of Prophecy

1. Try to avoid debt at all costs (*Counsels on Stewardship*, p. 257).
2. Sometimes debt is justifiable (*The Adventist Home*, p. 394).
3. Do not incur debt just to indulge the children (*Counsels on Stewardship*, pp. 251, 252).
4. Excessive debt can be discouraging (*The Adventist Home*, pp. 374, 393; *Counsels on Stewardship*, p. 254).
5. A debt incurred should be paid (*Testimonies*, vol. 5, p. 180; *Counsels on Stewardship*, p. 254).
6. Deny yourself and save the money to pay off debts (*Counsels on Stewardship*, pp. 180, 257).
7. Do not use God's money to pay off debts (*Testimonies*, vol. 1, p. 220; *Counsels on Stewardship*, p. 92).
8. Debts do not excuse the believer from the duty to sacrifice for God's cause (*Testimonies*, vol. 1, p. 220; *Counsels on Stewardship*, p. 258).
9. Unpaid debts bring a reproach upon the church (*Counsels on Stewardship*, p. 255).
10. Once out of debt, arrange your finances so that you can stay debt-free (*Counsels on Stewardship*, p. 257; *The Adventist Home*, p. 393).

Getting Out of Debt and Staying Out

There are no quick solutions to getting out of debt. However, there are specific steps that the family can take once they have decided to get out of debt.

IT USUALLY TAKES A LONG TIME TO ENTER DEEPLY INTO DEBT; IT WILL PROBABLY TAKE A LONG TIME TO GET OUT OF DEBT.

Ten Steps in Getting Out of Debt

Step One: Commit your life to the Lord.—This first step is the most important. It recognizes that you are not in this struggle alone. God can provide the comfort and support that will help you come to grips with your financial status. It will also make it clear that you are His steward and the caretaker of funds He has entrusted to you. This first step will make all other steps easier.

Step Two: Take a complete financial inventory.—Sit down with the family and determine what the complete financial status of the household is. Take a financial inventory. Include all family income and all family expenditures. List the assets, their current value, and all the flows of expenses. Use the tables and material in this book to complete your inventory.

Step Three: Define what you mean by getting out of debt.—If you have 20 years of payments left on a 30-year mortgage and three years of payments left on a car note, it may not be realistic to think that you can quickly be completely debt-free without substantial new sources of income. Instead, set up definitions of what you mean by being debt-free. These may include short-term debt, consumer debt, credit card debt, or other specific types of debt. After you have listed your debts, indicate clearly which ones you want to be free of.

Step four: Set up a timetable for getting out of debt.—Set up an explicit timetable for when you will achieve certain goals toward getting out of debt. Develop a plan for the first year. Then make each additional plan on a year-by-year basis. Prepare an outline, projecting for no more than five years, of your long-range objectives. At the end of the first year, reassess your status and determine where you are on your goal. At the end of each year, readjust your goals as necessary.

Step Five: Return faithful tithes and offerings.—The first concrete action that you should take after determining that you want to get out of debt is to begin or continue the process of returning faithful tithes and offerings. Many families deeply in debt will stop or reduce the amount of tithe. However, for the Christian family this can be a mistake. Make God your partner. Return to Him what is due. Once this is done, then the problem of getting out of debt becomes God's problem, not yours. He has promised in Malachi 3:10 that He will open the windows of heaven to you. He even asks you to test Him. Armed with this assurance, continue to act in a prudent manner in order to get out of debt.

Step Six: Restructure your payments to meet your cash flow.—If it is necessary, contact each creditor and seek to restructure your debt with that creditor. This will ease your cash flow and keep you in the good graces of your creditors. It may also help keep your credit record sound. On one of your bills find the address of the person to talk to.

Step Seven: Establish a budget for all transactions.—Establish a budget for all transactions, including the return of tithe and offerings. After you have restructured the payments for your current debts, make sure that all future transactions strictly keep to that budget.

Step Eight: Go on a strictly cash basis for everything.—At this point, go on a strictly cash basis for all expenditures and financial transactions. Pay cash for gasoline, for clothes, for furniture, for everything. Use your checkbook instead of a credit card. Make no more bills until you have achieved your goal of getting out of debt. Even then, proceed with caution.

Step Nine: Cut up all your credit cards.—Cut up all credit cards—American Express, Visa, MasterCard, and all department store cards. Until your debt problems are over, do not use credit. Instead of a credit card, go to your bank and get a debit card. A debit card works like a credit card for all those times when cash or a checkbook is not appropriate. For example, you can rent a car with a debit card. However, a debit card requires that funds be on deposit with the issuing bank or institution. Then, whenever the debit card is used, funds are automatically subtracted from your account. With a debit card you will not establish any new debt.

Step Ten: Seek new sources of cash.—Seek new sources of cash through a second job, writing, a hobby, or anything that may provide additional money. However, do not refinance through a second mortgage or a finance company for a consolidation loan. *Everything a consolidation loan can do for you, you can do for yourself through restructuring your bills.* The advantage is that you will not go deeper into debt to accomplish your objectives. You will also avoid high finance interest costs.

9

Credit: How to Get It, How to Use It

Excessive debt can be a problem. However, in order to obtain debt it is important to realize that having a good credit rating may be essential. In our society, the ability to obtain a loan or to borrow is determined by the credit rating given to the family.

CREDIT IS THE ABILITY TO BUY OR BORROW ON TRUST. IT IS CREDIT THAT MAKES IT POSSIBLE FOR THE FAMILY TO INCUR DEBT.

The proper use of personal credit requires a detailed and constructive examination of the factors that make up the debt. These factors include: (1) the purpose for the debt, (2) the interest rates charged, (3) the length of the debt period, (4) the amount of the debt, and (5) the current and future income base to support the debt. All these factors are taken into account by a lending organization when credit is applied for. It is even more important that the Christian family take these same factors into account when deciding to borrow or to get credit.

What Is the Credit Rating?

The credit rating is an assessment of an individual's ability to pay and the individual's past payment record of debt. It is a measure of the individual's responsibility. This is how it works.

All credit accounts are for the individual.—Each member of a family has his or her own credit file. By law, neither spouse is responsible for the credit record of the other. The only records that appear in common are those held in joint accounts. Real estate held jointly would show up on both accounts.

Credit accounts are automatically opened with any debt.—A credit account is opened whenever an individual begins an account with a local department store or receives a credit card. Once debt is incurred, a credit history begins. This history is a record of how promptly the debt is repaid or whether the individual fails to repay at all. The credit history is usually recorded at a central credit bureau, of which there are many across the country. Many credit bureaus are tied to the three major credit bureaus that gather information across the country:

Equifax Credit Bureau
Box 740241
Atlanta, Georgia 30374
1-800-685-1111

TRW National Consumer Relations Center
12606 Greenville Avenue
Box 749029
Dallas, Texas 75374
1-214-235-1200

Trans Union
Box 7000
North Olmstead, Ohio 44070

Any creditor/merchant can add information to your account.—Any creditor who is a merchant or a registered business may supply information to a credit bureau regarding how well an individual has paid his or her debts. In order for the merchant to do this, there must be an account between the merchant and the individual. Merchants can make mistakes, so it is in the interest of each individual to know what is contained in his or her credit record.

How is information posted to your record?—Usually entries to your credit record are posted once a month by a computer file submitted in your Social Security number by the merchant. Several key items are common to virtually all credit records: (1) current indebtedness, (2) frequency of late payments, and (3) judgments or defaults entered against the individual. In addition, the credit bureau will seek information on your employment and salary history. Not all information is updated correctly, and some of it may be currently incorrect.

What are your rights regarding your credit record?—Under the Fair Trade Act, each individual with a credit record has rights that must be respected.

- You have a right to obtain a copy of your credit report from any agency that reports your credit. This credit report must be provided free if you have been denied credit within the past 30 days. At other times you will likely have to pay for the report.
- You have the right to inspect anything that is included in your credit record and to challenge anything that is not accurate. Inaccuracies must be removed after you have provided proof that the entry is incorrect.
- You have the right to enter relevant information into your credit record, including any mitigating circumstances.

Other things you should know about the credit bureau.

- The credit bureau rarely has a complete picture of your financial condition. Even in the most sophisticated systems, information is often missing or out-of-date.
- Each merchant interprets the data differently, and it is the interpretation of the data that gives the individual a credit rating, not the information itself.
- When the credit history is bad enough, few merchants will give an individual additional credit.
- New credit can almost always be obtained. The price is often far higher interest rates, the use of a cosigner, or both.
- An individual who has always paid cash for purchases does not have a credit rating and may find it difficult to get credit.
- Entries on your credit file will remain for at least two years; some entries will last even longer.

Having obtained a good credit record, the Christian family should guard it well through prompt payments. A good credit record is a valuable addition to good financial management.

What to Do if You Have Bad Credit

If because of a set of circumstances you find that you have bad credit, don't despair. Credit records are dynamic and changing. A bad credit record can be changed into a good or even excellent record. It will take time and patience, but there are ways that you can remedy this situation. Below are several concrete steps you can take to repair a poor credit record.

- Stop whatever practices you have had that have led to the poor credit record. Start immediately to pay all bills on time.
- Get a new credit report from all the major credit bureaus.
- Make an appointment with the credit bureau to determine what can be done about the credit record.
- Contact all creditors who have provided negative information, and try to get the information modified or withdrawn.
- Review all your financial records in the event there is a dispute regarding items on the file.
- Itemize in writing all changes that you want made to your record; provide proof for these changes. Challenge all items that you believe to be inaccurate.
- Place into your credit record any mitigating information regarding your credit record. Review your credit records each month for the next six months to make sure that changes have been made.
- Keep detailed records of all correspondence with the credit bureaus, and file a complaint, if necessary, with the:

  Federal Trade Commission
  Attention: Correspondence Department
  Room 692
  Washington, D.C. 20580

Conclusion

For the Christian family, debt is sometimes a useful way to enjoy a healthy financial life. With debt we are able to purchase homes in which to raise our children; cars in which to go to and from work, church, and other activities; and furniture to make our lives comfortable.

But debt used unwisely can be a drain on the spiritual as well as the financial condition of the family. To as large an extent as possible, the Christian family should try to avoid debt. When that is not practical, then debt must be controlled. Should it get out of control, the Christian family should look to the strength of its relationship to God and the intelligent means of ending the destructiveness of excessive debt.

Like a good name, Christians also will guard well their creditworthiness. It may come in handy.

10

Savings

Families need savings for

- unexpected trips
- emergency repairs to houses or cars
- school expenses
- braces
- down payment on a house
- down payment on a car
- 101 unexpected financial needs

Few items are as important for sound family planning as setting aside some portion of the family's income for savings or investment. Additional funds are thus available for some emergencies and for deliberate future expenditures. Savings are also available for the proverbial rainy day should the family's normal income be reduced. When a family has a sound savings plan and sticks to it, there is less pressure to act in an imprudent way with regard to finances. For such families there is less of a temptation to compromise Christian beliefs and standards, because the financial status of the family is sound. Such a family can more easily undergo the hardships associated with sudden loss of income and emergency financial needs than is the family without this resource.

The family should make every effort to have an adequate amount of savings to meet special needs. How much you should have at any single time will depend on your goals and the family situation.

Credit is often used as a substitute for savings, but it is not. For some purposes, like the down payment for buying a house or car, credit usually will not substitute.

How Much Should You Save?

When setting up its savings plan, the Christian family may consider using the following steps:

- Determine whether it is saving for an unanticipated event, a rainy day, or both.
- Establish an overall goal for the amount of money it wishes to have at a certain time in the future.
- Develop the habit of setting aside a fixed amount periodically, rather than trying to put aside a large amount at one time.
- On an annual basis, review the family's savings status relative to its changing needs.

THE FAMILY SHOULD SAVE ENOUGH TO MEET POTENTIAL EMERGENCIES. THIS MAY BE AS MUCH AS THE EQUIVALENT OF THREE TO SIX MONTHS' INCOME.

The goal of saving up to six months of your regular income is an interesting goal, but often not very realistic. Few families can truly save that much of their income—or can they? Suppose a family sets as a goal to save 30 percent of its annual income during a 5- or 10-year period. How much would it take? Before we discuss how much it will take, let us review the important concept of interest compounding and its effect on savings.

For each period a savings program is in effect, there will be returns as measured by interest, capital gains, dividends, or profits. This is:

TOTAL SAVINGS = MONEY SET ASIDE + RETURNS

Returns are usually measured on an annual basis and as a percentage of the amount of money set aside. Clearly, the family will strive for the largest reasonable return for a given amount of risk. Interest compounding means that both the amount originally set aside and the returns are reinvested in the next period. Therefore, during the second period the total amount of the savings/investment is equal to:

TOTAL SAVINGS = (ORIGINAL SAVINGS + ORIGINAL RETURNS) + NEW RETURNS

This process continues for every period that the savings program is in effect. The result is that returns are earned not only on the original investment but also on the returns from the reinvested original returns. This is the power of compounding discussed in chapter 2. It is emphasized here again as part of a savings plan. The essence of how savings are accumulated is: *steady, slow growth.*

For a savings program there are no shortcuts. While this sounds easy, the average family may find that it cannot set aside a regular amount each and every month, year in and year out. Situations change. There are increases and decreases in the amount of income available. Emergencies arise, and the savings program is often the first to suffer.

While it is comforting to know that money set aside can grow to become so much in such a short time, it is somewhat discouraging to discover how difficult it is to discipline the family to stick to the required pattern. If a savings plan is to be successful, there must be discipline.

A 30 percent savings plan.—Suppose your income is $35,000 a year. A 30 percent savings amount would be $10,500. In order to get that much into savings, you will need to set aside $141.96 a month for five years, or $57.01 a month for 10 years. These funds would need to be invested at 8 percent annual return, compounded monthly. Table 20 shows details of the amount of monthly savings required for incomes from $10,000 to $100,000 at intervals of $5,000.

The role of inflation.—It is important to realize how a savings plan will also be impacted by inflation. Inflation reduces the purchasing power of money. As a result, the true value of a savings plan is slowly being eroded. Thus, while a savings account will not face a loss in principal, it could subject the family to loss of purchasing power. For example, many savings plans return as little as 5 percent in annual interest. Yet, if the inflation rate is 6 percent, then there is an annual loss in purchasing power that is equal to 1 percent of the amount saved. Except in years when the inflation rate is very low, the family is steadily losing purchasing power under most savings programs.

However, all is not bleak. Inflation drives up the cost of the goods and services that we buy, but it also drives up the rate of earnings received by workers. In fact, since 1954 wages have tended to double every seven or eight years. Therefore, while $80 per week was viewed as a good salary in 1958, the average wage earner 30 years later earned more than $360 per weekfour times more. Under a prudent savings plan the Christian family will increase the amount it saves as its income increases. The family that five years ago was setting aside $100 per month should be able to set aside a higher amount today.

Table 20
Amount of Monthly Savings to Achieve 30 Percent of Annual Income

Annual Family Income	30% of Annual Family Income	Savings Amount Each Month		Your Savings Plan
		5-Year	10-Year	
$10,000	$ 3,000	$ 40.56	$ 16.29	
15,000	4,500	60.84	24.43	
20,000	6,000	81.12	32.58	
25,000	7,500	101.40	40.72	
30,000	9,000	121.68	48.87	
35,000	10,500	141.96	57.01	
40,000	12,000	162.24	65.16	
45,000	13,500	182.51	73.30	
50,000	15,000	202.79	81.45	
55,000	16,500	223.07	89.59	
60,000	18,000	243.35	97.74	
65,000	19,500	263.63	105.88	
70,000	21,000	283.91	114.03	
75,000	22,500	304.19	122.17	
80,000	24,000	324.47	130.32	
85,000	25,500	344.75	138.46	
90,000	27,000	365.03	146.61	
95,000	28,500	385.31	154.75	
100,000	30,000	405.59	162.90	

SOURCE: Calculation by author. Note that all funds are invested at 8% compounded monthly.

While increasing the amount saved will not reduce loss of purchasing power, it will help the family make savings a constant portion of income received.

Pay yourself first.—Find your approximate annual income and then determine whether you can save the required amount each month. There is a special trick to achieving this.

AFTER TITHE AND OFFERINGS, PAY YOURSELF EACH MONTH. WRITE OUT A CHECK AND SEND IT TO YOUR SAVINGS ACCOUNT.

This amounts to treating your savings as you would a special bill. Pay yourself. Make savings one of your regular bills. Treat it like you treat all other bills, except that it goes for *you*. Once this habit is started, it will not be long before you have achieved your savings goals.

Forms of Savings

Savings accounts.—Banks and savings and loan associations are the principal depositories of savings. Up to $100,000 in any one account is protected by the Federal Deposit Insurance Corporation (FDIC) or the Federal Savings an agency of the federal government.

Saving accounts in such institutions are as safe as money can be. Thus, savings accounts have the following characteristics: (1) safety, because the deposits are insured; (2) liquidity, because the money is almost instantly available; but (3) low rates of return, thus having the potential for loss of spending power. However, savings accounts can be increased at any time and in any amount.

Savings bonds.—Savings bonds originated with World War I and were a means for federal borrowing to help pay for the war. However, they have long since become institutionalized and represent a major form of savings for many families. Bonds can be bought through payroll deductions at most places of employment, and this has been an attractive feature for many.

There are two basic types of U.S. government bonds: Series EE and Series HH. The Series EE bonds come in denominations with values from $25 to $10,000, with a maximum purchase amount of $10,000 a year. These bonds are sold at a discount from the face value. They pay no interest and must be held to maturity in order to get the full face value. Real interest payments are usually less than those obtainable under other types of investments. However, they are completely safe. The Series HH bonds range in face value from $500 to $10,000 and pay interest every six months until maturity.

Other savings instruments.—There are other U.S. government obligations that are used as a source of fixed interest returns. These include Treasury bills, Treasury notes, and Treasury bonds. These savings instruments have many restrictions that make them useful to only a small segment of Christian families. These include large outlays ($10,000 minimum for Treasury bills) and long periods of maturity. However, they offer very safe stores for savings because they represent obligations of the United States government.

Certificates of deposit.—The final fixed interest savings instruments are the certificates of deposit issued by banks. These certificates carry a fixed-interest rate but are not insured by any federal agency. In addition, they must be held to maturity or they will incur a large interest penalty (the principal will not be diminished, but the amount of interest paid will be reduced). Typical maturity is six months. However, CDs, as they are called, pay a rate of interest that is higher than that available under most other fixed interest savings instruments that have the same value. Even though the CDs are not insured, it is rare that any funds are actually lost. In this sense they are relatively safe.

Savings, Investments, and Gambling

It is useful to make an early distinction between savings, investments, and gambling. There is much confusion about what these differences are.

SAVING, INVESTING, AND GAMBLING ALL INVOLVE SETTING MONEY ASIDE AT ONE OR MORE POINTS IN TIME WITH THE GOAL OF HAVING THAT MONEY INCREASE. ALL THREE INVOLVE RISKS AND RETURNS.

Given the preceding definition, it is clear that there are similarities among saving, investing, and gambling.

For many Christian families, the only sound practice is savings—that is, to place money in a bank or financial organization and let it draw interest. Then when it is needed, it is withdrawn from that institution.

Investments are sometimes viewed as speculation and therefore not proper

Christian practices. And we condemn gambling. What makes the difference?

The first difference comes with the degree of risk that the original amount of money invested will be lost.

Savings, we will be shown later, involve almost no risk of loss of the dollar amount put aside. The interest paid on a savings account is fixed—therefore the returns are known in advance.

Investments involve more risk than savings, but are associated with the possibility of a higher return on the amount set aside. The returns on investments are not known in advance, but can be anticipated.

Gambling involves the greatest risks of all. There is only a small chance that the individual will gain more than what is lost, but gambling may result in large returns to the amount set aside.

Are productive activities going on?—Another difference involves whether productive activity comes from the use of the money. For example, money set aside in a savings account at a savings and loan association is used to lend to those who would buy houses, build businesses, or help in the flow of goods and services. Most investments, though not all, also enhance productive activity. By this means, the economy can grow, and the general community is made better off.

Gambling, however, exists to serve its own purpose, which is to take money from one set of individuals and transfer it to another set of individuals on the basis of chance. With gambling a few get a large return, and the vast majority get nothing.

Why gambling is an unacceptable practice.—It is this last difference that makes gambling an unacceptable practice for the Christian family. It is a wasteful activity that robs, without the production of any good thing. It is associated with the worst excesses of greed, the seeking out of gain, and the establishment of mammon ahead of God. To the Christian family who acknowledges the supremacy of God, His ownership of all that the family owns, and the family's role as steward, gambling has no place in its financial plan.

GAMBLING IS ANY SCHEME THAT SEEKS TO PROVIDE EXTRAORDINARY WEALTH IN A SHORT TIME WITH ONLY A SMALL INVESTMENT.

The only way such a scheme can work, since no productive activity is involved, is through taking from many and giving to few. All lottery schemes, all "circles of gold" schemes, all chain letters, may be added to betting on horse racing, sports, cards, and games of chance as unacceptable gambling activity. If the family has any doubt about whether or not to engage in an activity that is presented as an honest activity for Christian involvement, then the following questions should be asked: 1. Is any productive activity going on—that is, will this activity lead to an increase in useful goods or services? 2. Does this activity promise increased money through steady, consistent growth, or is it a get-rich-quick scheme? 3. Does my gain come about only if someone else loses?

"Finally, brethren, whatsoever things are true, whatsoever things are honest, whatsoever things are just, whatsoever things are pure, whatsoever things are lovely; if there be any virtue, and if there be any praise, think on these things" (Phil. 4:8, KJV).

Summary

Savings have a major role to play in the financial plan for every Christian family. Savings provide for easy access to cash and may be used for anticipated or unanticipated needs. To prepare for unanticipated needs, the family should set a goal of having from four to six months of net income in its savings portfolio.

Savings should be placed in a safe and sound source that provides for safety of the principal as well as modest growth. Savings funds should also be highly liquid, that is, easily converted into cash. A reasonable target for savings is to place 5 percent of gross income into savings or investments.

Some savings banks or associations are insured by state agencies or not at all! The prudent family will weigh the risk of not being so insured against any additional interest such banks may pay. Many have lost their savings by placing them in an account not federally insured.

11

INVESTMENTS

Investment is "the use of money for the purpose of making more money, to gain income or to increase capital or both" (Jerry Rosenberg, *Dictionary of Business and Management*, 2nd ed.).

Investments are far different from savings, even though they both involve setting aside money for growth and future use. With savings, the only consideration is the method of the savings and the amount of interest that is to be expected. For the Christian family there is little need to spend large amounts of time trying to decide how best to save. Either the family makes the decision to save or it does not.

This is not true of some, if not most, investments. A major characteristic of investments is that they all involve risks of some kind. There is no certainty that a positive return will be made on the amount invested. Indeed, there is no certainty that most, if not all, of the principal will be intact when the invested funds are needed. Sadder but wiser is the man or woman who has lost all because of foolish investments. And such individuals are not rare.

SAVINGS INVOLVE RETURNS WITH RETENTION OF PRINCIPAL. INVESTMENTS INVOLVE POTENTIAL FOR NEGATIVE RETURNS AND NO RETENTION OF CAPITAL.

In general, savings involve no risk of principal. Investments, however,

- run the risk of loss of principal.
- run the risk of loss of purchasing power.
- run the risk of total loss of principal.

Some investments even involve negative returns, in that more is lost than the principal amount that was invested, leaving the investor in debt. In order to understand investments, it is important that we understand the various types of investments and their major characteristics. This is shown in Exhibit 14.

Exhibit 14
Summary of Major Investment Programs

Category/ Name	Description	Expected Return	Type of Risk	Safety of Principal	Liquidity
A. Fixed-income investments					
Treasury bonds—Series HH	10 years to maturity. Bonds sold at face value. Minimum $500 investment. No secondary market.	Low	Interest rate risk Inflation risk	Very safe	Very liquid
Treasury bonds	5-plus years to maturity. Bonds sold at face value. Minimum $1,000 investment. Active secondary market.	Low	Interest rate risk Inflation risk	Very safe	Very liquid
Treasury notes	1-7 years to maturity. Notes sold at face value. Minimum $1,000 investment. Active secondary market.	Low	Interest rate risk Inflation risk	Very safe	Very liquid
Treasury bills	3-12 months maturity. Bills sold at discount (less than face value). Minimum $10,000 investment. Active secondary market.	Low	Interest rate risk Inflation risk	Very safe	Very liquid

Category/ Name	Description	Expected Return	Type of Risk	Safety of Principal	Liquidity
Municipal bonds	Varied maturity. New bonds sold at face value. Minimum $5,000 investment. Type of bond varies by municipality and purpose. Active secondary market.	Medium	Interest rate risk Default risk	Safety depends on the munici-pality and its bond rating	Liquidity may vary
Corporate bonds	Varied maturity. New bonds sold at face value. Minimum $1,000 investment.	Medium to high	Interest rate risk Business risk	Varies by corpora-tion and type of bond. Some very risky.	Varied liquidity
B. Variable-income investments, common stock					
Blue-chip common	Ownership interest in major corporation. No minimum re-quired. Active secondary market. May provide dividends.	Low to high	Business risk Market risk	Principal at risk	Very liquid
Growth company, common stock	Ownership interest in emerging and growing com-panies. Usually provides no dividends, but high capital gains potential.	High	Business risk Market risk	Principal at risk	Very liquid

Category/ Name	Description	Expected Return	Type of Risk	Safety of Principal	Liquidity
Small company common stock, penny stock	Ownership interest in small company and investment in stock with very low stock price	Low to high	Business risk Market Risk	Principal at risk	May not be very liquid
Utility income stock	Ownership interest in utility or other company that pays high dividend yield. Limited capital gain potential.	Medium	Business risk Market risk	Principal at risk	Very liquid
C. Mutual funds (best described by their objectives)					
Aggressive growth	Stocks of emerging or very undervalued companies	High	Market/ Business risk	Low to moderate	Liquid
Growth	Stocks of established, growing companies	High	Market/ Business risk	Low to moderate	Liquid
Growth and income	Stocks of established, growing companies that pay dividends	High	Market/ Business risk	Moderate	Liquid
Income	Stocks of companies that pay high dividends	Medium	Market/ Business risk	Moderate	Liquid
Bond	Emphasis on corporate bonds	Medium to low	Interest rate risk Market risk	Moderate	Liquid

Category/ Name	Description	Expected Return	Type of Risk	Safety of Principal	Liquidity
Municipal	Emphasis on municipal bond	Medium to low	Interest rate risk Market risk	Moderate	Liquid
Money market	Emphasis on current income and high safety by investing in short-term securities	Low	Interest rate risk	High	Liquid
D. Real estate investments					
Own home	Ownership of prinicipal residence	Low to high	Inflation	Moderate	Limited liquidity
Rental property	Ownership of rental units	Low to high	Inflation Market risk Business risk	Low to moderate	Limited liquidity
Limited partnership	Passive investment in properties, chosen and managed by others	Unknown	Inflation Market risk Business risk	Low to moderate	Not very liquid
E. Speculative					
Collectibles	Ownership of commodities expected to rise; i.e., rugs, precious stones, artworks	High	Inflation Market risk Business risk	Low	Limited

Category/ Name	Description	Expected Return	Type of Risk	Safety of Principal	Liquidity
Stock and index options	Highly leveraged, short-term equities that provide options to buy or sell stocks	Very high	Market risk Business risk	Very low	Liquid
Futures contracts	Highly leveraged, short-term promise to buy or sell commodities, currency, or securities in the future	Very high	Market risk Business risk	Very, very low	Moderate liquidity

GLOSSARY

Nominal return	The rate of return on an asset without adjusting for inflation
Real return	The rate of return on an asset after adjusting for inflation
Expected return	The average, or expected, return on an investment calculated over the range of likely returns
Safety of principal	The likelihood that the original amount invested will be returned intact
Liquidity	Ability to quickly convert an asset into cash, at close to the market value of the asset
Interest rate risk	A change in the rate of interest such that the market value of the asset is reduced in value
Inflation risk	A change in the nominal rate of inflation in a way that reduces the real value of an asset
Default risk	The risk that the maker of a bond will cease to make interest payments and/or default on the return of the principal
Business risk	The risk that the business operation will turn against the company
Market risk	The risk that the stock market as a whole will go down, taking individual stocks with it

Investments may range from the modestly secure to the speculative and highly risky. But for most forms of investments there is a simple iron rule of investing:

NO INVESTMENT IS CONSIDERED AS SAFE AS SIMPLE SAVINGS OR GOVERNMENT BONDS. THERE IS NO GUARANTEE ABOUT THE AMOUNT OF RETURN THAT WILL RESULT. ALL INVESTMENTS HAVE AN ELEMENT OF RISK.

Why Make Investments?

Given all these attributes of investments, why do families invest rather than simply save their money? The simple reason is that families make investments because there is usually a larger expected return from an investment program than from a savings program. As long as you expect your average return during those years, even with negative returns, to be greater than the returns on savings, you will be better off investing.

Families invest for a variety of reasons. To some degree investments are made because they permit families or individuals to become actively involved in the investment process. For example, consider some of the reasons individuals invest in real estate, stocks, bonds, or their own business:

Exhibit 15
Reasons People Invest

Individuals often invest in	Because of
real estate	a desire to be involved in land, houses, property, and seeing things created from ground up
stocks	a desire to test their ability to understand the business world
bonds	a need to have a steady stream of income of a fixed amount, with some possibility of capital gains
business	creative urges; the desire to produce something

Attributes of Investments

To be successful in investing, you must understand the types of attributes needed for different types of investments and the types of attributes that you have. For example, real estate investments often involve creative activities that require the skills of the investor. Because of the challenge and creativity possibilities as well as the greater return, families frequently turn to investments in addition to simple savings.

All Investments Take Time

One important attribute of investments is that *all investments take time*. This includes (1) time for the invested funds to accumulate and (2) the amount of time the investor spends planning and watching over the investment. Depending on the nature of the investment, the amount of time spent by the investor can be considerable. More personal time is needed than is true of savings because there is more uncertainty in investing than there is in savings. Hard decisions often have to be made, but they should be made only after extensive study and, one would hope, prayer.

CHOOSE ONLY AN INVESTMENT PROGRAM FOR WHICH YOU CAN DEVOTE THE TIME NECESSARY TO MAKE SURE YOU ARE SUCCESSFUL.

All Investments Involve Risk

There are several different types of risks in an investment program. They include interest risk, loss of principal risk, and inflation risk. However, for the purposes of this book, risk in an investment program is defined as the likelihood of loss of the capital invested. One of the most misunderstood aspects of any investment program is risk and how it fits into that program.

Since all investments involve risk, the essential issues are how much risk should be assumed and what is the relationship between risk and return. The investor must clearly understand the riskiness that the total investment will be lost. There are few "can't lose" investments. Business deals can turn sour; real estate can cause the loss of more than the original investments; stocks can decline in value; in a hundred and one ways money invested can be lost. It is the uncertainty about how an investment program will turn out that makes investments risky.

How much risk can you take?—The family's or investor's ability to absorb the potential consequence of risk, that is, the "taste" for risk, is a major factor in the type of investment vehicle that is used. Some investments are by their very nature highly risky, yet have the potential for large returns. The taste for risk is an indication of the amount of risk the family is willing to assume in order to achieve its investment goals. When there is only limited taste for risk, safety and the maintenance of the principal are paramount. When the taste for risk is slightly greater, the investor is more willing to take chances, including the loss of principal, if that is necessary to achieve the investment goal.

When risk-taking becomes gambling.—However, when the risk of loss is large enough, investment becomes first speculation and then gambling. Thus, land is sometimes bought on speculation—the hope that it will later appreciate in value. Indeed, any commodity, security, or item of value whose purchase involves considerable risk but offers the chance for large gains is speculation. Such speculation is often the same as gambling. Because of the potential corrupting influence of speculation, it should be avoided by the Christian family.

Individuals must know their risk tolerance.—Each individual or family that undertakes an investment project must understand clearly its risk tolerance. There is usually, but not always, a direct relationship between risk and return. To some degree, the greater the return, the greater the risk. You cannot receive a greater than normal return to a particular type of investment without assuming a great deal of risk. Also, you must know how much loss you can tolerate when you make your investment.

IF AN INVESTMENT OPPORTUNITY PROMISES A GREATER THAN NORMAL RETURN, LOOK OUT! IT MAY BE TOO GOOD TO BE TRUE.

Knowledge of an Investment Project Is Essential

It is essential that you know something about the nature of the investment project you are preparing to undertake. This means reading up on the investment project, talking to others who are involved in this type of investment, and getting information from professionals in the business. Preferably, you should get information from more than one professional.

IF YOU DO NOT KNOW MUCH ABOUT THE INVESTMENT PROJECT YOU ARE UNDERTAKING, YOU WILL LOSE MONEY!

Objectives of an Investment Project

The first task for the Christian family when setting up an investment plan is to establish investment objectives. There are likely to be major differences between the Christian family and the non-Christian family in the investment objectives set. The Christian family usually has less interest in getting wealthy in this world's goods. Instead, investments may be a means to live a more comfortable life, to plan for the education of children, to prepare for retirement, or to advance the work of the church. Thus, this section will not examine get-rich-quick schemes or investment alternatives that would call into question the Christian's major allegiance.

Major types of investment objectives.—There are many objectives that the family may establish for its investment program:

- becoming financially independent
- eliminating all short-term debt (everything except a home mortgage)
- planning for retirement
- meeting future college expenses for children
- planning for major purchases (house, car)
- improving the standard of living
- passing on estate to descendants
- using for gifts to others, including church
- providing employment opportunities for others
- expanding the talents or interests of a member of the family

The family may choose one or several of these objectives for its investment program. Some of these objectives are for the short term, some for a longer period. Some investment objectives are focused on a steady increase in wealth, whereas others focus on income. Still other investment programs are designed for transfers to descendants or institutions after the husband or wife has passed away.

Short-term versus long-term objectives.—Some investment programs are deliberately short-term and designed to achieve a specific objective. If this is true of your family, then there are several short-term investments that have a relative degree of safety but higher than normal returns. However, most investment programs tend to be designed for the long term. If the family wishes for a short-term limited objective growth in investments with high safety, it may be best off with a savings plan. For most investment programs, the family needs to think in terms of five to 10 years or more, depending on the type of investment program selected.

Clearly, then, the Christian family will want to consider an early investment program that is designed for such things as educating children. When a child is 15, that is a little late to set up an investment program for a college education. Under those circumstances, a savings program may be more appropriate.

Growth versus income objectives.—An investment program can be chosen to provide steady growth so that after some period of time, there is a sizable increase in the family's assets. Alternatively, the family may want to use an investment program to supplement income from wages and salaries. Finally, an investment program may be chosen with the goal of preparing for retirement. Depending on the reason, some investment instruments are more useful than others. A *growth-oriented* investment may mean that there will be a few funds available for current consumption. Conversely, an *income-oriented* investment may mean a reduced growth rate. This is because growth is fastest when the investment returns are plowed back into the investment.

Transfers of income or assets to others.—An investment program may be established to provide transfers of income or wealth to children, grandchildren, or institutions such as the church or a school. Such an investment program, by its very nature, has a long-term objective. However, many families do not start an investment program to meet these types of objectives until other more immediate objectives are met. The Christian family should be aware that because of the magic of interest compounding, this type of investment objective should be started relatively early. Many children or institutions have been greatly blessed because someone bought stocks, bonds, or land and let them grow and mature for as long as 30 or even 40 years.

INVESTMENT OBJECTIVES ARE NOT LIKELY TO BE MET IF THE FAMILY DOESN'T UNDERSTAND ITS OWN AND GENERAL INVESTMENT CONSTRAINTS AND RULES.

How Liquid Do You Want to Be?

Liquidity means the ability to convert an asset into cash. Some investment assets, like government bonds, are extremely liquid. Others, like real estate, may require a long time to convert. In reality, virtually any asset can be converted to cash—if the price is right. If the family wants to sell real estate very quickly, it will be necessary to lower the price. In choosing an investment strategy, a family will need to determine how much liquidity it will require. Any investment portfolio should include some assets that can easily be converted into cash.

What Is Diversification and Why Is It Important?

The best way to explain diversification is with the expression "Don't put all your eggs in one basket."

Prudence and good stewardship require that to the extent it is able, the family should diversify its investment portfolio. If the family has a large number of investments, diversification becomes easier. However, if the portfolio is small, then diversification becomes more difficult, even though it is more important.

Diversification takes on two forms: (1) diversification *across* investment instruments and (2) diversification *within* an investment instrument. Diversification across investment instruments means that an ideal portfolio will contain real estate, stocks, bonds, and money market funds. Diversification within an investment instrument means that a stock portfolio will contain several different types of stocks.

How diversification works for different groups.—Diversification of a portfolio will depend on the particular family situation at a point in time. Young families will need a different type of portfolio than will a retired family. Because of their capacity for risk, some families will want to take a more aggressive approach to investing than will other families. For an example of models of diversified portfolios, take a look at Table 21. In this table three portfolios are presented: conservative, medium, and aggressive.

The conservative portfolio places more of its resources in fixed-income investments and income stock. The aggressive portfolio places more of its resources in stocks in general and in growth stocks in particular. The medium portfolio is a mix of the two. As might be expected, young families are more likely to adopt an aggressive, growth-oriented portfolio. If there are unexpected losses or less than sterling growth, the family has time to recover. However, an older family may choose to take the more conservative income approach to portfolio diversification. Such a family will not want to take undue risks with its resources.

All families are advised to consider carefully just what type of diversification it wants in the portfolio it has. However, all portfolios should be diversified in some way.

Table 21
Models of Diversified Portfolios

Instrument (expected annual return)	TYPE OF PORTFOLIO		
	Conservative	Medium	Aggressive
Money Market (4-6%)	30%	20%	10%
Stocks (10-15%)	30%	40%	60%
Income (8-10%)	20%	20%	20%
Growth (15-20%)	10%	20%	40%
Bonds (6-10%)	30%	30%	20%
Real Estate (5-15%)	10%	10%	10%
TOTALS	100%	100%	100%

Separation of Living Expenses and Investments

An absolute must when considering an investment program is the complete separation of living expenses and invested funds. An investment program must come from funds that are left over after all living expenses are taken care of. If the family is starting to spend money targeted for living expenses for investments, then the investment program is not properly set up. In other words: *Never invest the rent money!*

Maintenance of principal.—Fundamental to an investment program is the goal of maintenance of principal. This means that if an investment program involves $5,000, then at all times the investor should seek to have at least that amount in the account. There could still be a loss, since the principal may be maintained but the buying power could be reduced. However, when the principal starts to diminish, the family may have to consider whether the investment program is prudent. Since any reasonable investment program is a long-term one, there may be occasions when the principal is reduced, but this should be the exception, rather than the rule.

There are tax advantages that need to be taken into account.—Different investment strategies yield different tax implications. For example, real estate investments can involve tax savings through depreciation, common stocks will involve capital gains or losses, and business ownership can have varied tax implications, depending on the form it takes. The tax savings can determine whether an investment is prudent or not. However, it should be noted that if an investment program is not inherently sound, it is usually not a good investment for tax savings purposes. Every investment has implications for tax savings or tax expenditures. Before undertaking an investment program, the family should consult a tax expert regarding the likely impact on the family's tax burden.

Calculating the Return on Investment

The rate of return on investment is an average annual percentage change in the value of an asset. It is the major indicator of the success of an investment program. The return on investment is measured in both *real* and *nominal* amounts. Real returns are adjusted for inflation, whereas nominal returns are not.

The *total return* on an investment is:

[(Net Amount of Returns) / (Purchase Price)] x 100

To calculate the *net amount of returns*:

(Current Value of Investment + Dividends or Interest) - (Principal Invested + Expenses of Investment + Taxes on Returns)

To determine the *purchase price*:

The purchase price is called the "basis" for the investment and is the historical cost of the asset.

To approximate the *annual rate of return*:

Divide the amount calculated above by the number of years that the asset was held. (This is only an approximation.)

To determine the *real rate of return* on investment:

Subtract the average annual inflation rate from the approximate annual rate of return.

Why calculate the annual rate of return on investment?—The formula and the definition seem formidable, and you may wonder why so much effort has gone into defining them and specifying what the returns are. The reason is that many families are unaware of just what is happening to their investments once they have been made. Many believe that they are earning a fair return on their investments when, in fact, the return may be far less than can be realized with a simple savings account or certificate of deposit that has virtually no risk of loss of capital.

It is important that the family use these figures and understand how to determine the return on investments if those investments are to be prudent. After there has been an introduction to several investment alternatives, these formulas shall be made more meaningful.

Conclusions

Given the above, how does the Christian family choose an appropriate investment program? The family should consider the following factors when deciding which investment program to set up:

- skills or interests of the family
- access to financial capital
- taste for risk
- amount of funds available to invest
- amount of end-money desired
- involvement of family or friends

The key to any investment program is to choose an activity that is consistent with the skills or interests of the family or the member of the family who will take the lead in the investment activity. Remember that investments require time, involve some risks, and involve far more thinking than do savings accounts. It is important that the family have some skills or the ability to acquire those skills before venturing on an investment program.

The family is encouraged to use the public library to find out more about investment alternatives, because only a limited presentation is made here. There can be more than one savings or investment strategy. Indeed, there is every reason for the family to have a savings account regardless of whether or not it decides to go into investments. It is also prudent financial planning to diversify into several investment alternatives.

Whatever choices are made, they should be made only after much prayer, family discussion, extensive reading about the nature of the investment (using books readily available in the library), and consultation with acknowledged experts on that investment approach.

Properly developed investment programs, although involving a degree of risk, can be consistent with Christian principles. The concepts examined here should help the family make prudent decisions.

As the Christian family gives itself over to its investments, they could become an all-consuming passion, even robbing God of time that is His. Thus, as the family contemplates investment, prayerful consideration must be given to the amount of time that those investments will take. The Christian family must be prepared to give up any investment or investment activity that distracts from the major goals and objectives of being a Christian. If investments are the most important things in the Christian's life, then it is time to give up those investments, regardless of what they are.

12

INVESTMENT IN FIXED-INCOME SECURITIES

The concept of investing in fixed-income securities has a pleasant ring to it. The investments are made, the income from the investment is known, and the principal remains intact. In addition, fixed-income securities may require far less personal care and attention than would other forms of investment. For the Christian family that wants to keep its risks to an acceptable level and minimize the amount of time spent on an investment, this may seem like the perfect type of investment. But all investments have some degree of risk. Also, there are many types of fixed-income investments. The issue is how to get the best features of a fixed-income investment program while seeking to achieve the family's overall objectives.

What Is a Fixed-Income Security?

A fixed-income security is primarily a federal government, municipal government, or corporate bond. It may also take the form of a note. The holder of the bond or note is a creditor to the issuing entity. The bond is a promise to pay a fixed rate of interest until the bond matures, and then the issuer promises to return the face amount of the bond.

A FIXED-INCOME SECURITY IS ONE THAT PROVIDES A FIXED, GUARANTEED RETURN ON THE INVESTMENT MADE OVER THE LIFE OF THE INVESTMENT.

All bonds have three crucial features:

Coupon rate: the face value interest payment rate

Maturity date: the date that the bond is to be redeemed
Expected risk: the likelihood that the issuer will default

The *bond coupon rate* does not change during the life of the bond. Thus, if a $1,000 face amount bond has a 10 percent coupon rate, then the bondholder will receive $100 each year in interest income *and* the return of the principal amount of $1,000 when the bond matures. The *maturity date* may range from a few months to as many as 20 to 30 years. The *expected risk* of a bond is the likelihood that the issuer of the bond will default on the bond.

If all bonds were bought for face value and held to maturity, then decisions on whether or not to buy bonds would be relatively simple. However, because new bonds are continually being issued and interest rates fluctuate regularly, the price of a bond on the secondary market will vary—sometimes widely. This is important for at least three reasons: (1) the family may need to sell the bond before the maturity date; (2) the price of the bond may vary because the rate of interest may have changed dramatically since the time the bond was first purchased; (3) sometimes the family's investment program changes.

Let's explore each of these circumstances and derive some implications for the family.

The family decides to sell its bonds.—A family may have many reasons it may decide to sell its bonds before the maturity date. The unexpected need for cash, the desire to use the bond funds for other types of investments, and the occurrence of the investment objective (the start of a child's college career) are three of many such reasons. There is an active secondary market for bonds of every maturity date and coupon rate. Therefore, the family should have little trouble selling the bond. But what price will the family receive? If the family receives less than the principal amount it invested, then there will be loss of principal—something the family sought to avoid by buying a fixed-income security. On the other hand, the family could actually receive more for the bond than it originally paid for it. Any reputable bond dealer will tell the family how much it will receive for its bonds. This is the bond price.

The price of a bond changes.—The value of a bond, or its price on the secondary market, is determined by the size of the annual interest payments and the amount of time until the bond matures. The interest paid on bonds in the secondary market is compared to the interest paid on newly issued bonds (which reflects the current interest rate). The price of the bond is then adjusted so that it sells *at a discount* (less then the face value of $1,000), *at par* (equal to $1,000), or *at a premium* (more than the face value of $1,000). This is summarized in Exhibit 16.

Exhibit 16
Relationship Between Coupon Rate and Bond Values

IF THE COUPON RATE IS	THEN THE BOND VALUE IS
Less than the current interest rate	Less than $1,000
Equal to the current interest rate	Equal to $1,000
Greater than the current interest rate	Greater than $1,000

If the family purchased a bond when the coupon rate was 8 percent, for example, and the current interest rate is 10 percent, the bond must be sold for a discount. Why? If the family had $1,000 with which to buy a bond and one bond offered $100 per year in annual interest income and the other offered $80 year, which one would the family buy? Clearly, the one that offered 10 percent annual return. However, if the bond price is lowered so that the effective return, or yield, is the same, then it would not matter to the family which bond it bought. Therefore, when such a bond is old, it must be sold at a discount. Conversely, if the prevailing interest rate is less than the coupon rate of the bond, the bond will sell at a premium.

There is more than one yield of a bond.—There are two important yields of any bond. One is the *current yield* or coupon yield. It is the amount guaranteed as an annual interest payment. The other yield is called *yield-to-maturity.* Yield-to-maturity reflects the fact that even though bonds may sell at a discount or a premium, when they mature the face value must be paid. The yield-to-maturity is the bond market's way to reflect the effects of the discount or premium. A simple relationship will make this clear:

YIELD-TO-MATURITY (OLD BOND) = YIELD-TO-MATURITY (NEW BOND)

All that this is saying is that for a given level of risk, the bond market continually adjusts the true yield, or yield-to-maturity, by changing the price of the bond until the above relationship holds true. Note that the coupon rate remains the same but that the price changes.

Why Are Bonds Rated?

Bonds are rated on the likelihood that the issuer will default (go bankrupt), making the bonds practically worthless or certainly reduced in value. The higher the rating, the safer the issuing agency or company is believed to be. Also, on average, the higher the rating, the lower the coupon rate the issuing agency or company has to pay.

Two companies—Moody's and Standard and Poor—have developed rating systems for virtually all municipal and corporate bonds. Bonds with high ratings generally pay the lowest coupon rate. Thus, U.S. Treasury bonds, rated as the safest bonds (if the U.S. government defaults or goes bankrupt, then we are all in trouble!), pay the lowest coupon rate. At the other extreme, high-yield or "junk" bonds are those with high-default risk. These bonds pay coupon rates that are much higher than U.S. Treasury bonds. Nevertheless, many issuers of high-yield bonds have never defaulted on their bonds.

What Are Municipal Bonds and Are They Right for You?

More than 14,000 local government entities, like cities, school districts, water districts, etc., issue bonds. Like corporate bonds, these are rated and provide a coupon that is based, to a large degree, on their rating. It should be noted that few municipalities have ever defaulted on their bond payments. What makes municipal bonds especially attractive is that their interest payments are exempt from federal taxes. Depending on the marginal tax bracket the family is in, municipal bonds can provide a good source of safe, secure income—although the rate is not very high.

Putting It All Together

Fixed-income investments can provide a relatively safe, secure form of income to the Christian family. Because the income is fixed, the family can more easily plan on how much it will have available as income or for future use. However, if there are changing interest rates—especially if the rates go up—the family can suffer loss of some of the principal if it must liquidate some or all of its bonds. Because only a few families hold bonds to maturity, the potential volatility in bond prices must be considered when the family is deciding whether to invest in bonds.

Which Bonds Should You Choose?

There are literally thousands of bonds that can be part of a fixed-return investment portfolio. How is a family to choose from among them? As always, the objectives of the investment and the amount of risk the family wishes to take are all ingredients in the decisions about which bonds to purchase.

Table 22 lists a representative set of government, corporate, and municipal bonds from an issue of the *Wall Street Journal.* These rates are illustrative and will vary depending on economic conditions, market conditions, and a host of other factors. To get current details, see a local business journal. This list illustrates several facts about bond rates. They will vary, but, surprisingly, by not as much as one might think.

Table 22
Recent Yields on Fixed-Return Investments

Type of Investment	Maturity	Yield
A. U. S. Treasury Bonds and Notes		
February 1994	1 year	3.86%
February 2000	7 years	6.50%
February 2015	22 years	7.38%
February 2021	28 years	7.44%
B. Corporate Bonds		
Chase Manhattan (Baa2/BBB)	8 years	8.20%
Citicorp (Baa3/BBB+)	9 years	8.50%
Pacific Gas & Electric (A1/A)	5 years	7.48%
Amoco (Aaa/AAA)	14 years	7.91%
C. Municipal (Tax free)		
California Public Works	14 years	6.36%
Georgia Municipal Power	12 years	6.20%
LA Dept. of Power and Water	30 years	6.28%
Washington Public Power	13 years	6.51%

The data show that a family can choose fixed-return bonds with a variety of rates and maturities. It is possible to invest for up to 30 years and receive a 7.5 percent return on a risk-free investment. There are also high-yield bonds that yield as much as 20 percent. However, they have a higher risk of default. In general, you can get a return that ranges throughout most investment objectives. To select the bonds that are best for your family, careful research is definitely required.

13

Stocks as Investments

For many Christian families ownership of corporate stocks and bonds are too much like total involvement with the world. For some it is capitalism personified and representative of the love of money. Unfortunately, for many individuals stocks are a gamble with the goal of getting rich and enjoying this world's goods, thus helping give stocks the aura of speculation.

Of itself stock investment is simply a means of ownership in a publicly owned company. There is nothing about stock ownership, per se, that violates Christian ethics. Stock sales enable companies to raise money for expansion. There are very strict public disclosure requirements made by the United States Securities and Exchange Commission regarding information on companies that wish to trade stocks publicly.

Advantages of Holding Stocks

There are several advantages to holding stocks:

- The dividends paid by most of the major companies provide a steady source of income to the holders of the stocks.
- The appreciation in value of many stocks are a hedge against inflation and often enable a family to accumulate for future needs.
- Stocks can be purchased in very small amounts and held for as long as the family chooses.
- Stocks have great liquidity, and the stock of major companies can be disposed of almost instantly.
- Stocks held over time have consistently outperformed other forms of investments, including bonds and money market funds.
- If chosen properly, stocks can have relatively limited risks.

Possible Dangers and Pitfalls

The potential investor must be aware of many possible dangers and pitfalls in buying and selling stocks.

- Stocks can go down in value as rapidly as they go up. For stocks of some lesser-known companies, there is a real chance that almost all the investment will be lost.
- Some stocks offer a far inferior return on the investment than such low-risk investments as certificates of deposit or even savings accounts.
- The timing of stock purchases and stock sales can make the difference between a successful investment and one that is not.

STOCKS CAN INVOLVE GREAT RISKS, AND IN ORDER TO INVEST SUCCESSFULLY THE INVESTOR MUST HAVE MORE KNOWLEDGE ABOUT WHAT IS GOING ON THAN IS TRUE OF OTHER COMMON INVESTMENTS.

Stock investments take time. Unless the Christian family is careful, stock involvement can consume large amounts of time that could best be devoted to more suitable Christian pursuits. If the Christian family is prudent regarding its investments, stock ownership can be part of an investment portfolio.

Fundamentals of the Stock Market

Many good books on the operation of the stock market have been published. The Christian family that is contemplating such investments would be well advised to study such books carefully. What follows covers some of the most important aspects of the stock market.

What is a stock market?—Let's begin with the basics. A stock market is a highly computerized and centralized means of trading the stock issued by publicly owned companies. There are many stock markets.

Stocks are certificates giving the owner claims to the assets of the company. But don't take your shares and ask for your "piece of the rock." Stocks traded publicly are usually issued in the mega-numbers. For example, International Business Machines (IBM) has more than 600 million shares of stock outstanding. Even if you own 1,000,000 shares of IBM (worth more than $90 million), you would still have only 1/600 of the total votes. Major companies have stockholder equity in the billions of dollars with hundreds of millions of stock outstanding. Few families are ever in the position of owning more than just a few of these stocks.

Exhibit 17
The Major Stock Exchanges (Markets)

NYSE	The New York Stock Exchange (NYSE) is the major stock market in the United States. Stock of the largest and most financially sound companies trade on the NYSE. It is located near Wall Street in New York City.
NASDAQ	The National Association of Stock Dealers and Quotations (NASDAQ) is commonly called the "over-the-counter" stock market. This market operates strictly through computerized quotes. There is no central location.
AMEX	The American Stock Exchange (AMEX) is a smaller centralized stock market located in New York. Stock of smaller countries are traded in this exchange.
Other Exchanges	There are other exchanges located in Chicago, Denver, Philadelphia, Kansas City, San Francisco, and other cities. These tend to be lesser known and trade local or specialty stocks.

What does a share of stock entitle the owner to?—A share of common stock entitles the owner to:

- any dividends per share issued by the company.
- the right to exchange the stock at a price determined by the market for that stock.
- the right to transfer ownership of the stock.
- the right to vote as an owner of the company.

Most individuals are interested only in buying and selling stock. In the process, they hope that the stock will rise in price. However, there is much to be said for holding the stock for investment purposes. Also, the ability to transfer stock ownership means that the stock can be given as gifts to friends, relatives, or institutions.

There are thousands of companies that issue stock. In addition to the stock of the well-known, large companies, there are thousands of smaller, lesser-known companies that have publicly traded stock. Thus the investor has thousands of potential stocks in which to invest. Depending on when the investor buys or sells the stock, there may be gains or there may be losses. Determining which stock to buy, when to buy it, and when to sell it makes all the difference.

How do you make money in the stock market?—Stock investing is designed to help your money grow. It can do it in two ways: (1) through increases in value—capital gains—and (2) through dividend yields.

Exhibit 18

TYPE OF RETURN	DEFINITION
Capital Gain	The change in price relative to the price paid for the stock, shown as an annual percentage change
Dividend Yield	The amount of dividends paid relative to the price paid for the stock; shown as an annual percentage change

Capital gains are realized when the stock is sold. There may be a paper gain, but there is no taxable gain until realized through sale of the stock. The capital gain should be calculated on an annual percent basis. If the stock you own goes from $50 to $100, that is a 100 percent gain. However, if it takes 10 years to do this, it is only a 7.18 percent annual rate of return. Conversely, if it takes five years to do this, it is a 14.87 percent annual rate of return.

For successful capital gains, the old adage is: To be successful in the stock market, buy low and sell high!

Dividend yields result from the annual amount of dividends received relative to the purchase price of the stock. Some stocks will have dividend yields of 3 percent, 4 percent, 5 percent, or more. The dividend yield is shown each day for stock traded on the major exchanges in the business section of the *Wall Street Journal.*

Return on Stock Investment

On an annual basis the return to stock investing is:

PERCENT ANNUAL RETURNS = PERCENT CAPITAL GAINS + PERCENT DIVIDEND YIELDS

As an illustration of the potential return of a stock investment, consider an investment of $9,900 that is used to buy 110 shares of IBM at $90 a share. IBM pays a dividend of $4.84 per share a year, or 5.38 percent annual dividend yield ($4.84/$90). The $4.84 per share is $532.40 a year in dividends for the 110 shares.

If the price of IBM stock goes from $90 to $99 within the first year of purchase, there will be an annual capital gain of 10 percent and a cash gain of $990 for the 110 stocks. The total cash gain is $1,522 on a purchase costing $9,900. The annual percentage gain from the purchase of IBM is:

percent annual gain = 5.38 percent + 10 percent = 15.38 percent

Any comparison of the returns provided by stock investing must take into account both the dividend yield and the capital gains. Stocks should be chosen that will give the proper mix of these two, depending on the investor's objectives and taste for risk-taking.

The entire stock securities industry spends millions of dollars every year to find such an ideal mix. However, it is not easy to do. And remember, each time that someone is buying a stock, someone else is selling that same stock.

What is a Christian family to do? To begin with, let's take a look at some of the various types of stocks.

Types of Stocks

There are many ways to classify stocks. The companies may be old established companies or newer start-up companies. Some are well-known, whereas others are known only to a few investors. Three of the more popular ways to classify stocks are whether they are blue-chip, growth, or income stocks. These classifications are not unique, but they help provide some guidance in the types of stock available.

Blue-chip stocks.—Stocks known as blue-chip come from the strongest and best-known companies in this country. Companies like General Motors (GM), International Business Machines (IBM), Exxon (EON), American Express (AEP), and other such companies usually pay dividends and will have capital gains over time. For such companies there are only limited risks that they will go bankrupt, thereby causing the stock to fall in value. However, it should be noted that the stocks in this category may fluctuate widely throughout time.

Investors choose this type of stock because there is the possibility of receiving a steady increase in stock value while enjoying some dividends paid out of earnings. In addition, these companies tend to be steady performers. However, like all stock, they must be chosen carefully. Some blue-chip stocks soon cease to be so.

Growth stocks.—This is a class of stocks whose price is expected to grow at a higher rate than other stocks. These stocks are usually issued by companies that are newer and growing more rapidly. This type of company usually does not pay dividends, but its stock is chosen for its capital gain. There also is a greater risk of loss than with blue-chip stock. But if the stock in this category performs as anticipated, the returns will be larger than those of the more conservative blue-chip stock. Currently many biotechnology and high-technology companies fit into this category.

Investors choose this type of stock with the hope that there will be capital gains over a long period of time. These stocks are often associated with new technology (like biotechnology) or new fads (like clothing). Some stocks of this type make dramatic capital gains, often exceeding 50 percent in a single year. They also can make dramatic falls, often exceeding 50 percent in a single year. Let the buyer beware!

Income stocks.—This class of stocks pays a regular dividend as many as four times a year. The dividends are usually paid regardless of whether or not the company has earned a profit for that quarter. Perhaps the stock that best represents this group is that of the American Telephone and Telegraph (AT&T) company. Prior to the breakup of AT&T, this stock was known as the "widows and orphans" stock, since the dividends were so faithfully paid for those who needed income and a very small capital gain. As a result, AT&T continues to be one of the most popular stock holdings in the country.

Investors choose income stocks because there is some possibility of capital gain, but a known flow of dividends. Some companies advertise that they have paid dividends for decades. The clear implication is that they will continue to do so. If current income is important to the family's financial plan, then they will seek this type of stock.

The Stockbroker

All purchases and sales of stock must go through a registered stockbroker, who charges a fee for each transaction. The fee is based on the cost of the stock and the number of shares purchased or sold. The broker works for one of hundreds of brokerage firms licensed by the Securities and Exchange Commission.

The investor can choose one of two investment strategies when using a stockbroker. First, the investor can use the services of a *full-service broker*, who provides research and advice on which stock to buy and sell, as well as offering buy and sell services. The major brokerage houses, such as Merrill Lynch, Shearson American Express, Salomon Brothers, PaineWebber, and E. F. Hutton, can offer the full range of research on the various companies. They can give detailed information on past performance of any company traded on the major exchanges. However, the costs for each transaction are as much as 3 percent of the value of the transaction.

CHOOSE YOUR STOCKBROKER WELL. YOUR FINANCIAL HEALTH MAY DEPEND ON IT!

Alternatively, the investor can use one of the *discount brokerage* firms that do not provide research and advice. When using a discount broker, the investor does his or her own research. Few serious investors rely exclusively on the advice given by the stockbroker. Most spend time studying various companies, using such publications as the *Value Line Investment Service*, or other such service, to determine which stock to buy and when to sell. The cost of the discount broker usually is around 1 percent of the cost of the transaction.

Neither the full-service nor the discount broker can assure investors that they will make a positive return on their investments. No broker can guarantee that there will be a fair return on the investment. Therefore, the investor must be very prudent in how any stock investment is made.

What Is the Best Way to Get Started in the Stock Market?

Investing in the stock market has challenged many persons who have studied the market for many years. In this short book it is not possible to provide a complete strategy on how to invest in the stock market in such a way that there will be a superior return. There are, however, several things the family can do to ensure that it has a realistic chance of earning a fair return on stock market investment. In Exhibit 20 the major steps in getting started in the stock market are listed.

Exhibit 19
Steps in the Stock Investment Process

Step 1	*Prayerfully consider* where stocks will fit in your financial objectives. Involve the whole family.
Step 2	*Set up a set of goals* for the investment. Determine whether those goals are long-term (5 years or more), short-term (1 year or less), or for a middle term (1-5 years).
Step 3	*Buy no less than two* books that describe how the stock market works and the factors in prudent investing.
Step 4	*Determine how much* of your savings you want to put in stocks.
Step 5	*Set up a simulated* set of stock investments and see how well they work. Do this for at least 3-6 months, using imaginary money.
Step 6	*Shop around for two* stockbrokers; use both to determine how well you get along with either.
Step 7	*Invest carefully* and watch, but don't get too anxious.
Step 8	*Remember that stock* investing is a long-term proposition.

Diversification as an Investment Strategy

The investor should diversify when investing in the stock market. Diversification means that several different types of stock are chosen, as well as several different stocks with each type. That is, the ideal portfolio should have some blue-chip stock, some growth stock, and some income stock. Depending on the size of the portfolio, there should be at least 5 to 15 different types of stock within the family's stock portfolio.

What Is a Mutual Fund?

Few Christian families have a large enough portfolio to permit the purchase of many different stocks at a single time. Many others do not have the time or expertise to choose which stocks to buy or how to gauge whether or not the portfolio suits their needs. In these instances, the family may satisfy its stock market investment needs by making mutual fund investments.

A MUTUAL FUND IS AN OPEN-ENDED COMPANY OR TRUST THAT USES ITS CAPITAL TO INVEST IN THE STOCKS OR BONDS OF OTHER COMPANIES OR INVESTS IN MONEY FUNDS. IT ACCEPTS NEW INVESTORS AND REDEEMS INVESTOR SHARES.

For many families a mutual fund is the ideal way to invest in stocks, bonds, or money market funds. This is because mutual funds have the following attributes that make them especially attractive:

- professional money management
- diversified portfolio, by law
- numerous risk and reward combinations

Professional management.—The most attractive aspect of mutual funds is that they are managed by individuals trained to select stocks and bonds and to manage a diverse portfolio. However, one must be cautioned that the majority of such professionals do only a mediocre job of ensuring a return that exceeds just random choice. Many money managers have losses repeatedly year after year. *Professional management does not mean that there will be superior results.*

Diversified portfolio.—By law, all mutual funds must invest in a widely diversified set of stocks, bonds, or money market funds, depending on their stated objectives. Mutual funds advertise themselves as having certain objectives, including growth, income, and total returns.

Risk and reward combination.—The investor in a mutual fund can select among specialty funds that invest largely in banks, retailing, telecommunications, biotechnology, high technology, utilities, and any one of a number of funds that promise a specific combination of risk and reward.

What to Look for in a Mutual Fund

Load versus No-load.—A *load* mutual fund is one that charges a fee on the gross amount of your investment. A *no-load* fund does not. The fee can be as much as 8.5 percent of the gross investment. There is no consistent reason that the investor should pay a load for the investment. The returns of a no-load investment fund have been shown to be similar to the returns of a load fund.

Exit fee.—A no-load mutual fund may charge a fee to exit the fund or redeem shares. This fee will have the effect of reducing the ultimate returns to the investment, although it rarely reduces the returns to the same extent as the front-end load of a load fund.

Size of the investment.—Some mutual funds allow you to invest as little as $100 at a time, whereas others require as much as $1,000 for each investment. If you want to make small investments, it will be necessary to choose those mutual funds that permit it. Alternatively, you may wish to accumulate larger amounts in a savings account until such time as you are willing to make the larger investment.

Automatic investment from bank.—You might want to have funds automatically withdrawn from your savings or checking account. Then look for a mutual fund that permits that.

Switching ability.—Market forces change, and from time to time the family may want to switch from one type of investment strategy to another. Some funds will permit unlimited switching, whereas others will charge a small fee. This is not a major problem, but if the family makes frequent changes in strategy, it could be costly.

Summary

This chapter has introduced only some aspects of investing in the stock market. The Christian family need not be concerned that all such investing is an unacceptable type of investing, although some of it is. What is important is to realize that investing in the stock market is for those families who seek investments as a reasonable alternative. Over the long haul, stocks offer some of the highest returns on investment. But there are risks involved in investing in the stock market. It is not something that the family should do without much prayer, study, and prudence.

14

Risk Management and Insurance

Life presents a great amount of uncertainty. Living a Christian life does not preserve us from the onslaughts of random and capricious events. On any given day, we do not know what will occur that will cause major changes in our lives:

- a car accident
- the death of a spouse or parent
- hospitalization of a relative
- a house fire

Risk management and insurance are the principal means of coping with potential and real financial hardships that come from these major changes in our lives.

Risk Management and Faith

Is the use of risk management techniques a denial of faith? Hardly. Risk management is simply being prudent in our financial affairs. As will be shown in this chapter, the use of risk management techniques and insurance reflects prudence in the stewardship of the resources given to us by God.

RISK MANAGEMENT INVOLVES A PRUDENT APPROACH TO MINIMIZING THE ECONOMIC LOSSES THAT RESULT FROM THE OCCURRENCE OF UNDESIRABLE EVENTS.

There are many ways to introduce risk management into the financial planning of the Christian family. As identified in Hallman and

Rosenbloom's book *Personal Financial Planning* (New York: McGraw-Hill Book Company, 1983), there are four stages in the risk management process. These stages help us identify, minimize, and reduce the *economic losses* that could come from risks.

Stages in the Risk Management Process

Stage 1.—Identification of the family's exposure to risk requires taking inventory of where the family is vulnerable to incurring economic risks. Any family that owns a home or rents an apartment, any family that has a car, and any family that has a wage earner can be exposed to risks that lead to economic loss. In addition, risk exposure can be identified by:

- the lifestyle that the individual lives.
- animals or special equipment on the property.
- other special circumstances that have the potential for causing economic losses, either for the family or a stranger within the gate.

Stage 2.—The family or the individual can frequently avoid risk through prudence in how they manage their affairs. For example, storing oily rags in a basement area may lead to a spontaneous fire that destroys or seriously damages a house and endangers lives.

Another example of exposure to risk includes behavior such as high-speed driving on winding roads. Diet, associations, and choice of amusements are also frequently the sources of risk that could lead to economic loss. To the extent possible, the Christian family has an obligation to avoid those activities and behavior patterns that increase risk.

Stage 3.—When risk cannot be avoided, prudent risk management includes the use of deductibles in an insurance policy to share the potential economic loss.

Automobile and health insurance plans commonly contain a deductible clause in which the insured pays for the first few hundred dollars of a loss, while the insurance company pays all additional costs.

Deductibles, coinsurance, or copays permit the family to accept small losses rather than seek to transfer them completely through insurance. In most instances the insurance company will not cover the total loss. When this option is available, it usually means that the insurance premium is substantially larger.

Stage 4.—Some risks cannot be avoided. Whenever we drive a car, show up for work, or are just involved in living, we take risks that may lead to economic loss. To reduce the size of such economic loss, we can transfer risks through the use of insurance.

We insure our homes to reduce the economic loss that may come from fire, other types of damage, or injury to visitors. We insure our cars to reduce the economic loss that may result from damage to our car, to someone else's car, or to passengers. We insure against the economic loss that can result from sickness or disability. Finally, we insure for the economic loss that can occur to the remaining family in the event of the death of one of its members.

What should the Christian family protect?—Should the Christian family seek to protect against every event that could lead to economic loss? All such protection costs the Christian family money that could be used for other purposes.

Two basic concepts underlie the reasons for risk protection. First, we are stewards of all that has been entrusted to us. That stewardship includes conserving and protecting.

Second, there are certain needs that come with participating in a family. The family unit needs financial security to grow and mature. That financial security can come from the income brought into the home and the use of risk management to prevent the sudden loss of that security. When the family is left unprotected, an unanticipated accident or the sudden death of a wage earner can result in a financial catastrophe, thus leaving the family destitute.

Savings are not enough.—Savings alone are often not enough to shield the family from sudden, unexpected economic loss resulting from death, fire, sickness, or an accident. With enough savings, it is argued, insurance is not needed. That is, the family is self-insured. That may have been true at a time when financial risks were not as high as they are now. Today it is virtually impossible for the average family to save enough to cover the economic losses for the types of emergencies that may come up.

Fifty thousand dollars in savings cannot replace a house, pay for the medical costs of a long sickness, or provide for economic loss in the event of the death of a wage earner. Fifty thousand dollars can buy an annuity that pays only $5,444 per year for 20 years at an 8 percent rate of interest. Would that be enough income to support the family? But even so, how many families have even $50,000 in savings?

These considerations make it clear that risk management is a vital part of financial management for the Christian family.

Basics of Automobile Insurance

In most states special insurance is required if the person owns and drives an automobile. There is a large risk to the driver that he or she will be involved in an accident causing property or personal damage. The financial loss can include the driver's own car, property damage to another car, plus the financial and/or health and/or life loss of another party in the accident.

Even if you are not responsible for an accident, most jurisdictions will require a bond until a final determination is made as to who is at fault. In the absence of auto insurance, the family is exposed to needless financial loss.

DRIVING WITHOUT AUTOMOBILE INSURANCE IS FOOLISH RISK MANAGEMENT.

For example, if an uninsured driver is at fault in an accident in which a life is lost or someone is seriously injured, the judgment against the driver could easily exceed $100,000. For almost all Christian families, this would mean financial devastation. In addition, the injured party may suffer unjustly because of the absence of insurance to cover the cost of damage done by the Christian driver.

Under all circumstances, automobile insurance is a prudent part of risk management of the Christian family.

The basic parts of automobile coverage.—Automobile coverage consists of five basic parts: liability, medical, uninsured motorist, collision, and comprehensive.

Some parts of the coverage are optional.—Virtually all auto insurance policies contain those five parts. However, the insured need not buy all five. The insurance regulations of most states require only that the insured have provisions for liability—either property or bodily injury. This protects pedestrians or the other driver. Most insurance companies require that the driver have collision. This protects the insurance company. The uninsured motorist, medical, and comprehensive coverages protect the owner.

Liability covers both bodily injury and property damage to other persons when the insured contributes to or causes an accident. The amount of coverage is limited by the terms of the contract. The bodily injury coverage should be at least $100,000 per person and $200,000 per occurrence. This means that if you cause an accident, the insurance company will pay up to

$100,000 to the person injured and up $200,000 total for that accident.

Exhibit 20
Parts of Automobile Insurance Coverage

Liability	the legal liability of an insured for bodily injury or property damage for which he or she is responsible
Medical	the amount of reasonable medical and funeral expenses paid in the event of the injury or death of the insured
Uninsured motorist	payments made to the insured for personal or property damage caused by a driver who has no insurance; this covers both bodily injury and property damage
Collision	payments made by the insurance company to the insured to pay for repair of the insured's own car when the accident is caused by the insured
Comprehensive	payments made to cover the loss or damage to the car that are not the fault of the owner: theft, fire, vandalism, floods, or other such events

If the damage is severe and a judgment is made in excess of that, then the insured is liable. Clearly, these minimum amounts will protect the insured from catastrophic loss up to the limits. The greater the amount of coverage, the higher the premium for this portion of the insurance, but the less risk the individual incurs if there is a large judgment against him or her.

For some drivers it is advisable to carry up to $1 million in liability, and up to $500,000 in medical. The additional coverage is sometimes needed if the family is concerned about a large judgment. It is not uncommon for a jury or judge to award very large settlement amounts. Incredibly, the amount of the judgment does not depend on how much insurance coverage the individual has. In most jurisdictions the amount of insurance is not even taken into account. Clearly, a large judgment could devastate a family's financial status.

Medical coverage is for relatively minor injuries to you, passengers in your car, or pedestrians harmed by your car. The amounts of coverage are generally low, in the range of $5,000 for each person.

The *uninsured motorist* coverage protects you against the irresponsibility of motorists who are not insured and who cause property or bodily injury to you. Your insurance company will reimburse you for your losses up to the limits that your policy specifies. As a general rule, you should protect yourself at the same level that you protect the other driver in the event the accident is your fault. That means if you have coverage of $100,000 for the other driver, you should have $100,000 coverage against the uninsured driver.

Collision protection permits you to get your car repaired in the event it is damaged by you. Collision tends to be the second most expensive component of your insurance coverage. Clearly, you should insure cars that are relatively new or for which you still owe. However, the time may come when the coverage costs more than the car is worth. That is something that has to be considered in determining whether or not to provide collision coverage for the car. Collision is subject to a deductible ranging from $0 to $500 or more. This means that you will pay the amount of the damages up to the deductible; then the insurance company will pay the balance.

Comprehensive coverage cares for damages to your car caused by events totally outside your control. As is true for collision coverage, it is best for newer cars and may not be very practical when the car is old or worth relatively little.

Costs of Automobile Insurance

The costs of automobile insurance will vary with each insurer. In addition, for a given insurer rates will vary with the age, sex, driving experience, and previous claim history of the insured. Rates will vary with the type of car insured and whether the individual lives in a high-risk location or one that has had fewer insurance claims. Rates will vary across states and across jurisdictions within a state. Insurance rates are difficult to compare across insurers, and some insurers may not insure certain types of drivers (generally, those with excessive moving violations) or certain types of cars (very expensive or high-performance cars).

To help you comparison shop for the best insurance value for your car, use Table 23. Keep the conditions the same for each car, and find out from at least three insurance companies what the rates would be. Remember also that some insurance companies will vary by service delivered in the event you need them. Cost should not be the only factor, but it certainly should be the major one.

Table 23
Comparisons of Insurance Companies

Type of Coverage	Limits/Conditions	Comparison of Insurance Companies		
		#1	#2	#3
Liability	$100,000/$300,000			
Medical	$10,000			
Uninsured Motorist	$100,000/$300,000			
Collision	$200 Deductible			
Comprehensive	$200 Deductible			

Factors in Selecting an Insurance Company

The major factors in selecting an insurance company are (1) costs, (2) service, and (3) accessibility. Once the costs are determined, you should look into whether or not the insurer provides quality services in the event of accident. Such services would include prompt attention to your claim, reliable and quality repair allowances, and ease in resolving your problems. The insurer should also be accessible. You should be able to make your claims easily, get estimates of the damages and their costs readily, and receive your check quickly.

Homeowner's and Rental Insurance

What is now *homeowner's* insurance started out as plain old fire insurance. Many individuals continue to think of home insurance as just fire insurance, but this type of insurance has changed dramatically in recent times. Look at what has happened to fire insurance!

Homeowner's insurance protects the insured against economic losses involving the home. The family is protected from financial losses arising from fire, theft, the dog biting the neighbor, the skate that causes the neighbor's kid to break an arm, and even the cost of motel bills in the event the family has to use a motel while the house is being repaired after covered damage.

As is true of any insurance coverage, there are limitations, exceptions, and deductions so that the family assumes some of the risk. Homeowner's insurance is usually a needed addition to the risk management planning of the Christian family.

Exhibit 21
Homeowner and Rental Coverage

HOMEOWNER COVERAGE	
Basic Coverage	Fire, lightning, vandalism and malicious mischief, theft of personal property, glass, breakage, and personal liability
Deluxe Coverage	*Basic Coverage* plus: *Personal property,* including; electronic equipment, coins, and items lost while away; *Credit card loss; Rent and other expenses; Debris removal*
RENTAL COVERAGE	
Coverage of only the personal property of the renter	

There are several good reasons for the Christian family to have this type of insurance protection:

- The family needs to be assured of having a place to live.
- The family home will be mortgaged during most of the time that the family lives in it. The bank will usually require insurance coverage.

How much money should the Christian family invest in homeowner's insurance? For some this may represent a lack of faith and trust. For others it represents prudent financial management. There is always the risk that the family will become so attached to the possessions of this world that the more important issues will be neglected. When considering such insurance, you should remember that all this is temporary.

Health and Disability Insurance

The high cost of medical care in the United States is well-known to all families. A single medical emergency can cost tens of thousands of dollars. If a family member has to use the intensive care services of a hospital, the costs can easily exceed $10,000 per day. Medical services for the elderly may exceed $100,000 per year!

ALL FAMILIES SHOULD HAVE SOME FORM OF MEDICAL INSURANCE.

One family out of seven has no form of medical insurance. For such families the alternatives are to use a hospital for the indigent, rely on the Medicaid assistance provided by the federal and state governments, pay for their own medical costs, or do without medical care. Not all families are eligible for government assistance, and many others do not wish to become dependent on state assistance.

Fortunately, most employers provide medical insurance for their workers—usually at a subsidized rate. For such workers there is little difficulty getting and keeping medical insurance. If the benefits are not provided free, they are paid for with a relatively painless payroll deduction.

Exhibit 22
Types of Medical Coverage

Hospitalization	provides for hospital expenses on a per diem basis or for a maximum number of days; provides for extra hospital benefits (such as medications, use of operating rooms, and other such services); and for some outpatient services
Doctor's Visits	periodic visits to doctor's offices on an outpatient basis, but not including surgical procedures
Surgical	provides for surgical fees charged by physicians and anesthesiologists
Major Medical	provides for catastrophic medical claims that are not part of the basic coverage listed above
Long-term Care	provides for payment in long-term care facility for the elderly or disabled

Medical insurance for the family is provided in three principal ways:

- Medical Plan (MD)
- Health Maintenance Organization (HMO)
- Primary Provider Organization (PPO)

Medical Plan

Family members insured under a medical plan, such as Blue Cross/Blue Shield, may choose which physician and hospital they want to use in the provision of medical services. However, most of these medical plans contain some limitation or another.

For the basic medical plan the limitations are set either by the number of days that coverage is provided or by the dollar amount that will be paid for any particular medical need. Major medical coverage usually will not pay for routine doctor's visits that are not of an emergency nature.

Coinsurance.—Coinsurance refers to the amount of a medical bill that must be paid by the family. For example, a medical plan may be specified as an 80/20 plan. Under this plan the insurer pays 80 percent of the medical costs and the family pays the 20 percent balance. Another feature of coinsurance is the deductible. The first specified amount of the medical costs (for example, the first $200 per year) are paid by the family. The insurer then pays the balance. The higher the deductible, the lower the cost of the insurance premium. Of course, that means that the family pays a larger portion of the medical bill.

Coverage.—Medical coverage refers both to the types of medical needs and the individuals covered. Young families may choose to include maternity coverage, whereas older families that are past childbearing age would hardly have need for such coverage. Other specialized coverage may also fit the needs of particular families during selected periods of their lives. In general, only members of an immediate family or dependent children under 21 and living at home are included in a policy. However, a policy may be written for individuals, for husband and wife, for one family head and his or her children, or for the entire family.

Multiple coverage.—Many families have more than one medical coverage. This happens frequently when there are two or more wage earners and each employer provides medical insurance. When there are two or more insurance providers, there can be overlap of coverage. The result is that sometimes all medical costs are covered by one medical insurer or the other. However, medical insurers may refuse to cover some types of benefits if it is known that there are other insurers involved.

Health Maintenance Organizations

Health Maintenance Organizations (HMOs) provide a one-stop, comprehensive medical facility for major medical services. Choices of physician are limited in the HMOs, and the individual receives services from staff physicians.

The HMO may charge a small fee for routine visits or have other limitations. For some HMOs there is a wait for routine medical assistance, although all HMOs provide immediate attention to emergencies. In general, however, they are far less costly than the major medical plans.

Primary Provider Organizations

A Primary Provider Organization (PPO) is a collection of physicians who provide services for a fixed fee. Families that subscribe to this service choose one of the physicians from among the group. In some PPOs, the list of physicians is very large.

Like the HMOs, the PPOs require that the client choose from among a selected list of physicians. In the HMO the physician generally works exclusively for the organization. In the PPO the physician may also bill under various medical plans and may bill patients under Medicaid/Medicare.

Which Insurer Should You Choose?

Which of the many types of insurers should the Christian family choose for itself? The answer depends on the needs of the family, the costs, the medical status of family members, and the family's preferences for selecting their own physician.

The choice of which plan to use may be limited if the insurance is provided by the employer. Some employers, like the federal government, subsidize numerous insurance plans. Since there is no plan that is suited for all families, having many choices may prove beneficial to the family.

The Christian family must assess its needs for medical coverage, the availability of that coverage, the cost, and the expected medical needs of the family. All these things must be evaluated before the family chooses a particular insurer. But once such determinations are made, then medical insurance should be part of the risk management program of the family.

15

Risk Management Through Life Insurance

For the average family the greatest financial risk to be faced is loss of income because of the death of a wage earner. This is a risk to which all families are exposed. The family can avoid some aspects of this risk through prudent behavior, but it cannot be avoided entirely. In this instance, the use of deductibles will not be appropriate.

The loss of a loved one through death is a total loss. An economic loss occurs when income from the deceased was used to enhance or support the family. To make up the economic loss that accompanies death, the family has several options:

- absorb the financial loss.
- be self-insured through adequate financial reserves.
- transfer financial loss through insurance.
- collect Social Security survivor's benefits.
- collect means-tested welfare.
- increase the earned income work effort of the survivors.

In this chapter we focus on risk management through life insurance.

What Is Life Insurance?

Life insurance is a Risk Management Plan in which a contract is made between an insurer and the insured. The insurer agrees to pay a sum of money or any annuity to the benefactories in the event of the death of the insured.

There are several ideas in this definition that should be noted. First, life insurance is a risk management plan. Whether we wish it or not, there is a risk of death at any time for anyone from any of a number of sources. When there is financial dependency, death can cause major financial disruption. A financial plan that does not take this risk into account is not a complete plan.

Life insurance is a contract.—Life insurance involves a contract, which is the life insurance policy. This contract is between the insurance company and the owner of the insurance. The owner can be the insured or a third party. If it is a third party, there must exist a verifiable economic interest of the third party in the insured. What this means is that no one can own a life insurance policy against the life of a stranger.

Early in the history of life insurance in this country, it was common for unscrupulous persons to take out life insurance policies on total strangers, hoping for their early demise. The obvious problems with this system were soon recognized, and laws were enacted that required an economic interest. Direct relatives qualify automatically. Where a business interest is shown, a company may take out an insurance policy on the life of some of its key executives.

What is a beneficiary?—Unlike ownership, any person, organization, or selected entity can be the beneficiary of a life insurance policy. Designating the beneficiary of an insurance policy is totally at the discretion of the policy owner. Thus, the owner can designate a spouse, child(ren), or relative(s) as the primary and secondary beneficiaries. But the owner can also designate his or her estate as the beneficiary. (Since there can be sizable estate taxes when insurance goes into an estate, there should be compelling reasons for so designating the insurance proceeds.)

The church can be a beneficiary of a life insurance policy.—The owner can designate an organization, like the church, as the primary or secondary beneficiary of the life insurance contract. Indeed, the owner can designate a stranger as a beneficiary.

The prudent Christian family will choose carefully who is to be the beneficiary of any life insurance policy. Usually the surviving members are the beneficiaries. However, should there be no surviving beneficiaries, the life insurance proceeds would go into the estate of the insured, to be covered by whatever estate rules are in effect.

The amount of the life insurance policy.—The life insurance policy states the amount of insurance available under the plan. The policy can be for $5,000, $10,000, $100,000, or $1 million! The policy can be written in such a way that the amount of the funds that are to go to beneficiaries will change during the course of time. The amount of the policy will depend on the objectives of the owner, the relative wealth, and what the insurance needs are. Later we will discuss how one determines the appropriate amount of life insurance to purchase.

Conditions of the life insurance policy.—The policy explains the agreement between the insurance company and the insured. The policy states the conditions under which the death of the insured will be covered. All insurance policies contain clauses that nullify the policy if death is the result of suicide before the policy is one or two years old. There may be other conditions that limit or restrict how much the beneficiaries will receive once the insured dies.

Many a family in the midst of grief over a loved one has learned to its dismay that the terms of the insurance policy are not what the insured intended when the policy was purchased. Almost always it is to the detriment of the family.

ANY INSURANCE POLICY SHOULD BE READ CAREFULLY AND UNDERSTOOD FULLY BY THE MEMBERS OF THE FAMILY. IF THERE ARE ANY QUESTIONS REGARDING THE TERMS OF THE POLICY, THEY SHOULD BE EXPLAINED IN THEIR ENTIRETY BY THE AGENT OF THE INSURANCE COMPANY.

Purpose of Life Insurance

The three basic purposes of life insurance are (1) financial protection for dependents, (2) creation of an estate to be passed on to heirs, and (3) a means of forced savings.

Of these three purposes of life insurance, the first is by far the most important. Ultimately life insurance is really a plan to provide for financial relief for dependents upon the death of a provider. The other two functions are better handled by other financial assets. Because this point is so important, it will be expanded by considering four fundamental rules for the ownership of life insurance.

Exhibit 23
Fundamental Rules of Life Insurance

Rule 1	Life insurance is for the survivors, not the insured. Its major function is to help relieve financial distress caused by the death of the insured.
Rule 2	The appropriate financial distress that would result from the death of the insured should be carefully determined. This determination, in combination with all other resources, should then be the basis for the amount of insurance and who should be insured.
Rule 3	Life insurance should not be used as a means of making the survivors rich. Don't overinsure.
Rule 4	Comparison shop for the type of life insurance program that best meets the complete needs of your family.

Insurance Policies for Children

There are almost never good reasons to buy anything but limited amounts of insurance for children. The argument is frequently made that if a child is insured at an early age, this will guarantee that the child will always be able to get insurance. Another argument is made that an insurance policy is needed as a means of saving for a child's later education. Under normal conditions the child will be able to buy insurance for his or her own dependents once the child becomes an adult. An insurance policy, with returns that are generally 3 percent to 7 percent at most, is seldom an ideal investment vehicle to save for college.

A small amount of insurance may be desired to provide for funeral and medical expenses in the event of the death of a child. Using insurance on a child to save for that child's future educational needs is not a particularly good financial plan since there are far better returns that can be achieved.

Insurance for the Elderly

The elderly should almost always be self-insured or at least coinsured. The heart of this reasoning is that if an adequate retirement program is put into place, there is money in the estate of the deceased that will take care of the final funeral expenses. (These funds may not be readily available, thus making a small insurance policy necessary even for someone with a large estate.) Final medical costs may be covered by insurance. Because the children of the elderly are grown, there is no need to provide for their financial needs.

Thus, insurance needs as determined by financial dependence are greatly diminished. Where unusual circumstances dictate, those older than 60 may want to continue to pay the very high premiums required to continue life insurance. However, it usually is not prudent to have large insurance policies on those over age 65.

How Much Life Insurance Do You Need?

One of the more difficult aspects of life insurance is determining the amount of life insurance needed for each person insured. Since life insurance is a risk management plan, the first thing the family should seek to determine is the amount of financial distress to the family that the premature death of the person to be insured will cause. There are no easy guidelines in making this decision. Each family's circumstances will vary as will their insurance needs. Let us take them one step at a time. These steps are summarized in Table 24.

Immediate Expenses

There are two primary expenses and two secondary expenses that must be taken care of immediately. The primary expenses are for the funeral arrangements and for any uninsured medical expenses. While funeral expenses can be predicted, uninsured medical expenses are an unknown.

Estimate final funeral expenses.—Use placeholders to estimate final funeral expenses and any uninsured medical costs. For example, $6,000 (in 1992 dollars) may be more than adequate for funeral expenses, and $25,000 may be more than adequate for any uninsured medical expenses.

The family must decide what to do with the house.—The secondary expenses are the outstanding bills, including the home mortgage, if there is one. The family may wish to pay off all bills so that there is a fresh financial start for the family. The family may also choose to pay off the mortgage, but even here careful thought must be given.

For example, a recently purchased new home may not be as desirable with one of the parents missing. The family may decide to move to a smaller house or even change neighborhoods. Alternatively, the family may choose to treat the house mortgage as another bill to be considered as part of long-term expenses. This would permit the family to turn the insurance proceeds into an income-producing asset.

Table 24
Checklist for Determining Insurance Needs

1	EXPENSE ITEM	AMOUNT NEEDED
2	**IMMEDIATE EXPENSES**	
3	Final funeral expenses	
4	Any uninsured medical expense	
5	Payoff of mortgage on house	
6	Payoff of any other outstanding bills	
7	TOTAL IMMEDIATE EXPENSES	
8	**LONG-TERM EXPENSES**	
9	Replacement income (annuity amount)	
10	Future or existing educational expenses	
11	TOTAL LONG-TERM EXPENSES	
12	TOTAL EXPENSES (SUM OF IMMEDIATE AND LONG-TERM EXPENSES)	
13	**INCOME SOURCES**	
14	Earnings of surviving spouse	
15	Social Security	
16	Pensions	
17	Savings	
18	TOTAL AVAILABLE INCOME	
19	AMOUNT OF INSURANCE NEEDED TO MAKE UP DEFICIT (TOTAL EXPENSES – TOTAL INCOME)	

Many a surviving spouse has used insurance proceeds to open up a business that provided far greater financial security than the proceeds themselves. A conservative approach to estimating insurance needs is to include the mortgage payment with the thought that alternative uses can be made of these funds if the need ever arises.

Pay off all other bills.—The family should plan to pay off all other outstanding bills from the insurance proceeds. This will insure a fresh start and minimize the amount of income needed to continue to sustain the family.

Long-term Expenses

The long-term expenses of the family will depend on the number and ages of the children and the desired future financial status of the family. Long-term needs include replacement income for the family's daily living expenses and future education costs. Neither is easy to estimate.

Projecting daily income needs for an extended future period may be very difficult. At any time in the future the size of the family may change, the surviving spouse may remarry, tastes and circumstances may change, and there may be changes in the economic marketplace. A practical life insurance plan will help the family maintain a reasonable standard of living during the succeeding years after the death of the wage earner, taking into account the adjustments the family must make to the loss.

A LIFE INSURANCE PLAN MUST TAKE INTO ACCOUNT THAT THE FAMILY CAN UNDERTAKE MANY FINANCIAL CHANGES TO ADJUST TO THE LOSS OF THE LOVED ONE.

An Example of the Calculation of Family Insurance Needs

An example of the steps required to calculate thc family's insurance needs is given below. Suppose a family determines that it needs $1,000 per month for a period of 15 years after the death of a wage earner. How much insurance would be needed? The family must also guess what its average rate of return on the invested insurance proceeds will be. Suppose the proceeds are invested at an annual rate of return of 10 percent. How much insurance would the family need?

Table 25 shows the amount of insurance needed to assure that $1,000, $1,500, or $2,500 per month can be available to the family for 15 years if the proceeds for the life insurance settlement are invested at 10 percent. The inflation rate is shown as a low 4 percent and a high 8 percent. The net gain in the invested funds is the rate of return minus the rate of inflation.

Look carefully at the information in Table 25, because it provides essential information about how much insurance is needed. It shows that if the family needs an inflation-adjusted income of $1,000 per month for 15 years, it will need $168,000 in insurance proceeds (of other assets) under low inflation and $295,000 under high inflation. If the family need increases to $2,500 per month, the needed insurance amount goes to $419,000 under low inflation and a whopping $799,000 under high inflation conditions.

Table 25
Face Amount of Insurance Needed to Maintain Constant Purchasing Power for 15 Years

MONTHLY AMOUNT	INFLATION RATE	
	4%	8%
	Amount of insurance needed	
$1,000	$168,000	$295,000
$1,500	$252,000	$444,000
$2,500	$419,000	$739,000

NOTE: These fixtures assume that the proceeds are invested in an account that pays 10 percent per year, compounded monthly. There is a monthly drawdown on the balance of the account, and the account is exhausted after 15 years.

This table makes it clear that when there is a high inflation rate, far more life insurance is needed to maintain a constant living standard. But the monthly expenses need not include such extra expenses as college costs for dependent children. To figure out what those costs might be, you first must approximate what the current college costs are.

Go to chapter 7 and look up the estimates of current college costs. At $10,000 per year and $47,000 for four years, the future college needs will depend on when the child(ren) will go to school. If it will be five years before the child starts school, the total funds needed will be $63,000 ($47,000 x 1.34, the inflation factor). A calculation like this would need to be made for each child and added to the gross amount of insurance. However, scholarships and student loans can reduce these required amounts.

You are now ready to sum up the gross insurance needs for your family. For an illustrative family, it may look like what is shown on Table 26.

Table 26
Illustrative Insurance Needs Calculation

IMMEDIATE EXPENSES	
Funeral expenses	$ 4,000
Uninsured medical expenses	5,000
Mortgage payoff	60,000
Payoff of oustanding bills	7,500
TOTAL IMMEDIATE EXPENSES	$ 76,000
LONG-TERM EXPENSES	
Replacement income ($2,500 per month)	$419,000
Educational expenses	49,000
TOTAL LONG-TERM EXPENSES	$469,000
TOTAL NEEDS	$544,000

Were this the end of the story, it would appear that this family would need a great deal of life insurance on the primary wage earner—at great expense. However, every family has some assets and sources of income available to it that would change this picture dramatically.

Income for Meeting the Risk of Loss of Wage Earner

There are four major sources of income to meet the needs that result from the death of the principal wage earner:

- earnings of the surviving spouse
- survivor benefits from the Social Security program
- pension or retirement income
- savings or investment income

Earnings of the surviving spouse.—The earnings of the surviving spouse can be a major factor in the amount of insurance that the family needs. In many families both parents are working when a premature death strikes down one. A nonemployed spouse securing a job will lessen the amount of replacement income needed.

Payments from Social Security.—Perhaps the most common form of replacement income are the Social Security payments to which survivors are entitled upon the death of a wage earner. While it is not anticipated that Social Security alone will be sufficient, its benefit for survivors can be considerable. In addition, Social Security benefits are adjusted annually for inflation.

Social Security benefits can go to the survivors as a percent of the Social Security benefits of the deceased.

Table 27
Percent of Benefits Received by Survivors

CATEGORY	PERCENT OF BENEFITS
Widow or widower, age 65 or older	100 Percent
Widow or widower, age 60-64	71½ Percent
Widow or widower, any age with children under 16	75 Percent
Children under 18	75 Percent

SOURCE: Dale R. Detlefs and Robert J. Meyers, *1992 Mercer Guide to Social Security and Medicare.* Table 6, December 1991, William Mercer, Inc. (no city listed, ISBN 1-880754-92-4)

As Table 27 shows, a surviving spouse age 65 or older can receive 100 percent of the benefits to which the worker was entitled. In 1992 that amounted to a maximum of $1,296 each month. This amount is adjusted for inflation. (There is a clear relationship between the monthly earnings of an insured worker and the amount of Social Security to which the family is entitled.) The amount paid to a surviving spouse is separate from the amount paid to the surviving child under 18. Such a child will receive his or her own benefit check regardless of the status of the surviving parent. The total amount received by the surviving spouse and all children is subject to a maximum benefit.

As the following table makes clear, the family of a deceased worker is entitled to upward of $2,267 (1992 dollars) per month, depending on the past income of that worker. This income is available until the youngest child is 18 years old (or 19 years if the child is still in elementary or high school). Additional income becomes available to the surviving spouse when he or she turns 60.

Table 28
Monthly Earnings and Survivors Benefits

Average Indexed Monthly Earnings	Benefits for workers and their families		Benefits for survivors		Maximum family benefit
	Age 65 retirement	Age 62 retirement	Spouse alone and 65	Spouse with one child	
$1,000	$ 544	$ 435	$ 544	$ 816	$ 876
2,000	864	691	864	1,296	1,539
2,500	996	797	996	1,494	1,742
3,100	1,086	868	1,086	1,628	1,900
3,700	1,176	940	1,176	1,764	2,057
4,500	1,296	1,036	1,296	1,944	2,267

SOURCE: Dale R. Detlefs and Robert J. Meyers, *1992 Mercer Guide to Social Security and Medicare.* Table 6, December 1991, William Mercer, Inc. (no city listed, ISBN 1-880754-92-4)

How to Compute the Potentially Available Income

When all the potential sources of income available to the family are summarized, it is possible to modify the total insurance needs. For example, if the family has income support needs of $2,500 per month, it may get as much as $1,400 of this from Social Security. When a family receives $1,400 per month for 15 years from Social Security (which is indexed to the cost of living), this is the same as receiving $252,000 toward the amount of needed replacement income.

If the surviving spouse decides to work, then the Social Security benefits for him or her may be reduced, but not the benefit on behalf of the dependent child(ren). Thus, a potentially large amount of the replacement income can come from employment and Social Security.

Earlier we saw that the illustrative family needed $544,000 in replacement income once the principal wage earner died. Now we see that as much as $252,000 of that can come from Social Security income. An additional $108,000 can result from the surviving spouse earning as little as $600 net a month for 15 years. The result is an insurance need of $184,000.

Exhibit 24
Steps in the Determination of Insurance Needs

Step 1	Determine what the total gross needs are likely to be using Table 24.
Step 2	Estimate the amount of income from the major sources, including earnings, Social Security, savings, and other such sources.
Step 3	Calculate the net insurance needs.
Step 4	Adjust the calculation for changing family circumstances.

The needs of the husband and wife should be calculated separately.—The insurance needs for the husband and the wife should be calculated separately. This exercise will show that when the wife is a wage earner, the amount of insurance needed for her can be considerable.

The illustrations given here show how all facets of the family's financial status must be taken into account when the amount of insurance needed by the family is determined. Although few families go through this type of analysis to determine their insurance, the family should make certain that these calculations are made for them before they consent to purchasing an amount of insurance that may be too large or too small to meet their needs.

Before the Christian family considers how much insurance to buy, it is useful to examine the concept of "diminishing responsibility." This concept embodies the notion that insurance is really designed as a risk management tool in which the need for insurance is directly proportional to the responsibilities of the insured.

AT A YOUNG AGE THE NEED FOR INSURANCE IS GREAT IN ORDER TO PROTECT THE FINANCIAL NEEDS OF THE FAMILY. AS THE INDIVIDUAL MATURES AND CHILDREN LEAVE, THE NEED FOR INSURANCE DECREASES. AT THE SAME TIME, INCREASING SAVINGS AND INVESTMENTS REPLACE INSURANCE NEEDS.

The concept of diminishing responsibility incorporates the notion of self-insurance as the family accumulates assets. Thus as assets such as the house increase in value and decrease in the remaining mortgage, as investments and savings accumulate, and as other planning decisions come into fruition, the family's need for insurance declines. This is illustrated in Figure 8.

Figure 8
Concept of Diminishing Responsibility

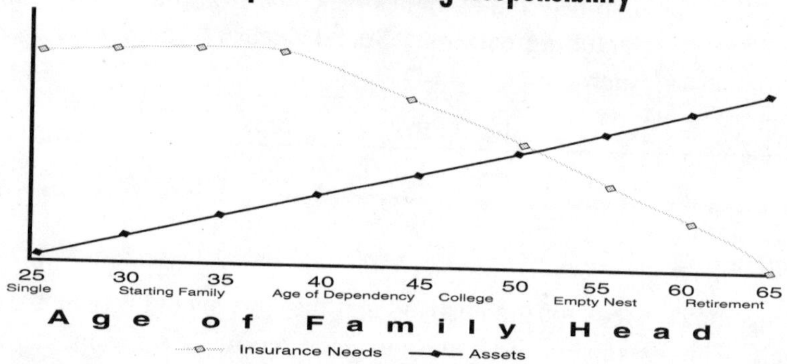

A man or woman who marries at age 25 will have only a limited need for insurance until children are born. Then the need is greatest, because should the father die while the children are still young, the mother would face huge expenses for raising and educating these children. This insurance need continues through the age of dependence but declines sharply once the children are no longer in the home—the "empty nest" period. By the time of retirement, at about ages 62-65, the only dependent is the surviving spouse in the event of death.

Table 29
Determining How Much Insurance You Really Need

Age of Head	25	40	55	65
Working Years left	40	25	10	0
Expected lifetime earnings	$1,600,000	$1,000,000	$400,000	$0
Ages of minor children	1-3 years	16-18 years	N/A	N/A
Total Social Security death benefit to age 65	$768,000	$288,000	$92,000	$800/mo
Gross insurance needs	$832,000	$712,000	$308,000	0

An example of how the concept of diminishing responsibility may be applied is shown on Table 29. In this illustration, the needs for insurance diminishes as the family head ages and as circumstances change.

Always remember the purpose of life insurance.—Remember, insurance is not designed to enrich heirs, but to act as a hedge against financial loss. As a married couple gets older and the children become independent, this responsibility fades. For those who wish to make the church a recipient of some parts of their estates, this can still be done through well-thought-out estate planning. During the time that insurance needs are declining, the prudent Christian family will have been building its asset position in anticipation of retirement. As these assets grow, there will be less financial burden should one spouse or the other die prematurely.

What Type of Insurance Policy Should the Family Buy?

There are four basic types of life insurance that the Christian family can buy. They vary in purpose, cost, coverage, and their acceptability for the family. Each has certain advantages and disadvantages, which are discussed below. The major types are summarized in Exhibit 25.

Term Life Insurance

Term life insurance policies provide coverage for a fixed period of time—one, five, 10, or more years—and then terminate.

This is the most basic type of life insurance. For the young family it is a means of providing the largest amount of insurance for the least amount of money. It is possible for the young family to insure one or both parents for $100,000, $200,000, $500,000, or even more for just a few hundred dollars a year.

Term policies come in two types:

- *Level period term.* Term policies in which the premiums remain constant for a specific number of years—5, 10, 15, or 20—and then the policy automatically terminates.
- *Decreasing term.* Term policies in which the premiums remain constant while the amount of insurance coverage decreases on a monthly or annual basis.

Some term policies are *renewable*, that is, they may be renewed at expiration without proof of insurability. At the time of renewal, the premium amount will be increased. Term policies may also be *convertible*, that is, they can be converted into whole life policies without proof of insurability.

Premium amounts.—Premiums for term insurance policies are determined by the expected likelihood of death of the individual. At young ages the likelihood of death is relatively low, so premiums are low. As the individual ages, the likelihood of death increases, so the premiums increase. This is illustrated in Figure 9.

Exhibit 25
Insurance Features at a Glance

Type of Insurance	Death benefits	Premiums	Dividends	Cash Value
Term	Fixed	Start out low but increase every year or every few years on a preset schedule	Paid on some policies; usually small	None
Whole Life	Fixed	High but usually stay constant	Paid on some policies; may be large	Rises according to preset schedule shown in policy
Universal Life	Can vary (within limits) at discretion of police holder	Fairly high but can vary (within limits) at discretion of policyholder	Typically none	Grows at variable rate dedpending on several factors, including the interest rate paid on the cash value, which the company can change from time to time
Variable Life	Can vary, but never dips below initial face amount	High; fixed	Typically none	Can vary depending on investments in underlying accounts

SOURCE: Trudy Liebermann, *Life Insurance: How to Buy the Right Policy From the Right Company at the Right Price* (Mount Vernon, N.Y.: *Consumer Reports* Books, 1988), Table 7.

Figure 9
Illustration of Cost Comparison of Term and Whole Life Policies

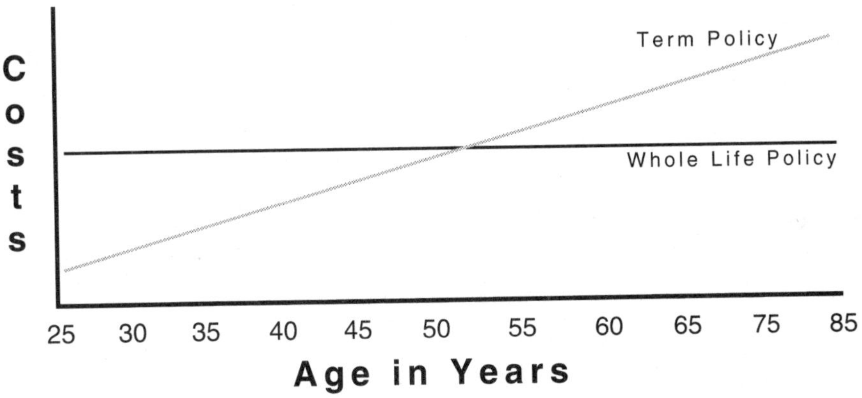

By the time the insured reaches age 65, premiums for term policies can become prohibitive. But, as will be discussed later, it is probably not necessary to have a large amount of insurance at that age.

Insurability.—Under the conditions of term insurance, the individual may be asked to prove that he or she is insurable. Being insurable means that there does not exist a medical condition that greatly increases the likelihood of death within the term of the insurance contract. Insurance companies may require a very large premium or may determine that the person cannot be insured.

*How much will term insurance cost?*An illustration of the cost of term insurance is given in Table 30.

Table 30 shows the insurance premium costs for a five-year renewable term insurance policy. The first year premium cost for a 25-year-old is $1.11 for each $1,000 in insurance. Thus, this 25-year-old can buy $100,000 in insurance for $111 for the first year premium. In years 2 to 5, the premium increases to $1.96 per $1,000, or $196 for the insurance costs from age 26 to age 30.

Between ages 31 and 35 the premium goes to $2.17, or $217 per year, for $100,000 in insurance coverage. Between ages 36 and 40, the premium goes to $289 per year, and by the time this person turns 41, the premium reaches $431 per year for the years 41 through 45.

Table 30
Illustrative Costs for Term Insurance Policy

	PREMIUMS FOR $1,000 INSURANCE				
Age at Start	First year	Years 2-5	Years 6-10	Years 11-15	Years 16-20
25	1.11	1.96	2.17	2.89	4.31
26	1.11	1.96	2.27	3.10	4.68
27	1.13	1.98	2.38	3.36	5.06
28	1.13	2.02	2.52	3.65	5.48
29	1.14	2.08	2.68	3.96	5.94
30	1.16	2.17	2.89	4.31	6.43
31	1.19	2.27	3.10	4.68	6.97
32	1.22	2.38	3.36	5.06	7.56
33	1.27	2.52	3.65	5.48	8.23
34	1.32	2.68	3.96	5.94	9.00
35	1.40	2.89	4.31	6.43	9.88
36	1.47	3.10	4.68	6.97	10.88
37	1.58	3.36	5.06	7.56	12.00
38	1.68	3.65	5.48	8.23	13.23
39	1.80	3.96	5.94	9.00	14.58
40	1.94	4.31	6.43	9.88	16.05
41	2.08	4.68	6.97	10.88	17.47
42	2.24	5.06	7.56	12.00	18.96
43	2.43	5.48	8.23	13.23	20.63
44	2.65	5.94	9.00	14.58	22.52

SOURCE: Actual payment plan for major insurance carrier.

At age 45 the individual pays premiums based on the attained age of 45. In this illustration the premiums will then go to $643 for $100,000 of coverage and will stay at that level until the person reaches age 50. At age 50 the premiums will increase to $988 per $100,000 and stay that way until the person reaches age 55.

At this point the law of diminishing responsibility starts to come into play. By age 55 the insured is likely not to have any children still at home. The financial responsibility drops considerably because there is no longer a need to educate children and care for the needs of the family for long periods.

This is also the interval during which family heads are not yet able to retire, so some insurance is still needed. But if the family has been developing a sound financial plan for retirement, there should be a sizable nest egg set up. The Christian family should then be moving toward self-insurance. By the time a person reaches 65 there should be full self-insurance. Cash should be available to take care of immediate needs, a small insurance policy may assist in some expenses, but the major part of the estate should consist of assets.

Employers frequently provide term insurance.—When insurance is employer-provided, it is almost always term insurance. Many groups, such as teachers, government workers, or workers in nonprofit organizations, are able to take advantage of relatively inexpensive term life insurance through an employer. These policies provide insurance that is a multiple of the individual's annual income. Because it is a group policy, proof of insurability is often not needed. The employee can make the payment through payroll deductions. However, if the worker changes jobs, the insurance does not travel with him or her. For most workers employer-provided insurance should be a supplement to the other insurance of the individual.

Whole Life Insurance

Whole life insurance policies are designed to remain with the person throughout his or her life or to age 100, whichever comes first. The premium amounts are fixed throughout the life of the policy and will not change. The policies do not have to be renewed, and once the person is approved for insurance, he or she can keep that policy as long as premiums continue to be paid. The death benefit of the whole life policy is the amount guaranteed to beneficiaries in the event of the death of the insured.

Because the premiums for whole life policies exceed the actual cost of insuring the individual, cash benefits accumulate and are invested. This *cash value* is the amount that the family will receive when the policy is cashed in.

How large are premiums for whole life policies?—Premium amounts for whole life policies are large, but remain constant throughout the life of the insured, up to age 100. The cost of insuring individuals increases with the increased risk of death (as the person ages). As a result, insurance costs tend to be very high when the person is young and needs the greatest amount of insurance, and relatively low when the insurance needs are less.

A 30-year-old man typically pays between $1,200 and $2,000 per year for a $100,000 whole life policy. The cost of term policies was $217 per year for the same person until age 35. In some instances insurance companies charge much lower premiums for the early years of a whole life policy, after which the policies increase.

The insurance costs for whole life policies vary greatly across companies, the age of the individual when the insurance contract is first started, and the various features of the individual policy. When shopping for whole life insurance, look carefully at the cost and the feature structure of several companies.

What is the cash value of the whole life policy?—Cash value is the amount that is available to the insured at any time that he or she wants to cash in the policy. Cashing in a whole life insurance policy means that the individual no longer has insurance coverage, but receives whatever cash has accumulated in that policy. Policies state the expected rate of the accumulation of cash value.

Individuals may choose to cash out whole life policies in order to become self-insured (typically at age 65) or to convert to another form of insurance. When the person cashes out the value of the insurance policy at age 65, it is usually to buy an annuity for future living expenses or to make separate investments.

An individual may choose to cash out a whole life policy in order to buy another form of insurance, such as a term policy. However, the insured should be careful to make sure that there is an overlap of coverage when the transition takes place. One of the worst things the Christian family can do is cash out a whole life policy because of its cost without immediately replacing it with an alternative form of insurance.

Dividends.—Insurance companies invest the premium income and pay out benefits depending on the mortality rate of the insured. In many instances the premiums exceed the need for payout. The excess premiums may be returned to the insured in the form of reduced premiums or even a check. In order to take advantage of these dividends, the insurance policy must be a *participating policy*.

You can borrow against your cash value.—One of the advantages of the whole life policy is that the insured can borrow against the cash value of the policy. This provides the individual with a ready source of cash without cashing in the policy. However, the amount of insurance coverage is diminished by the amount borrowed.

For example, suppose the individual has $25,000 in accumulated cash value in a policy that has a death benefit of $100,000. If the person borrows $15,000, the death benefit is reduced to $85,000. Once the person pays back the borrowed funds, the death benefit increases to its former level.

Cash value is gone in the event of premature death.—One of the disadvantages of a whole life policy is that the cash value that accumulates in the policy is lost to the family if the person dies prematurely. For example, let us suppose that the insured has a policy with a death benefit of $100,000 and an accumulated cash value of $25,000. If that person dies without cashing out the insurance policy, the family receives the $100,000, but not the $25,000 in cash value. Since the premiums for the $100,000 policy were higher than required for the insurance policy, the cash value is lost to the family.

Limited payment whole life.—Limited payment whole life policies are those in which the insured pays for a fixed period of time—usually 20 years—and then does not need to make further payments to keep the insurance in force, up to age 100. Such policies have the advantage that they require payments only for a short period. However, the premiums are much higher, since they must cover premium costs during those years that the individual no longer pays premiums. It may be a poor choice for a young family that needs large amounts of insurance.

Shopping for a whole life policy.—When you shop for a whole life insurance policy, there are several things to keep in mind:

- The premiums are not the only thing to look for when comparison shopping. Also look at the rate of cash value accumulation and the full range of benefits.
- Look carefully at the printout of the death benefit and cash value schedule prepared by the insurance salesperson. Ask to see several alternatives.
- Never buy whole life insurance without getting policy cost and benefit information from several insurers.

An example of a whole life payment schedule, death benefit, and cash value for a 35-year-old male is illustrated in Table 31. It shows that there is a constant annual payment of $1,980 for the rest of the life of the insured. In return the insured gets a constant death benefit of $100,000 and an increasing cash value. Should the insured wish to cash out the policy, the cash value is the approximate amount of money he or she would receive. At age 55 this would amount to $32,800; at age 65, this would amount to $46,400.

Table 31
Illustrative Features of Whole Life Policy for 35-year-old Male

End of Policy Year	Annual Premiums	Death Benefit	Cash Value
1	$1,980	$100,000	—
2	1,980	100,000	—
3	1,980	100,000	$ 1,500
4	1,980	100,000	3,100
5	1,980	100,000	4,800
6	1,980	100,000	6,500
7	1,980	100,000	8,200
8	1,980	100,000	9,900
9	1,980	100,000	11,700
10	1,980	100,000	13,500
11	1,980	100,000	15,300
12	1,980	100,000	17,200
13	1,980	100,000	19,000
14	1,980	100,000	20,900
15	1,980	100,000	22,900
16	1,980	100,000	24,800
17	1,980	100,000	26,800
18	1,980	100,000	28,800
19	1,980	100,000	30,800
20	1,980	100,000	32,800
Age 60	1,980	100,000	36,700
Age 65	1,980	100,000	46,400

SOURCE: Actual policy and premium for major insurance carrier. Policies vary greatly across carrier, time, and family circumstances.

Should you buy a whole life insurance policy?—For most Christian families the answer would be a resounding no. There are several reasons a whole life policy is not recommended:

- The premiums are too high for the level of insurance.
- The rate of increase in cash value is very small compared to alternative investments.
- If you borrow against your cash value, your insurance coverage is reduced by the amount you borrowed.

- Your family loses the cash value of your premiums should you die before the policy is cashed in.

All these reasons make a whole life insurance policy a questionable purchase for the Christian family.

Universal Life Insurance

In response to the dramatic fall in the amount of whole life policies written, the insurance industry developed what is called universal life insurance. These policies seek to provide a greater return on the invested premium while making it easier for young families to afford the large amounts of life insurance they need. The universal life insurance policy operates under a very simple principle:

CASH VALUE = PREMIUM PAYMENT – COST OF INSURANCE

Under this principle the insured selects the basic amount of death benefit, say $100,000. The insurance company then determines the pure insurance cost for that insurance, using an accounting calculation that is based on the likelihood of death at that age.

Next the insured makes a large initial payment to start the policy and then determines whether or not to pay an increased premium above the amount stipulated. The insured also determines whether the excess of the premiums over the cost of insurance should go into cash value or to increase the death benefit.

Finally the insured has the option of missing some premium payments, letting the premiums be paid by the accumulated cash value. However, this has the effect of seriously eroding both the death benefit and the cash value. The illustration in Table 32 shows how the universal life insurance concept can work.

In the examples in Table 32 the individual who takes Option A receives a level death benefit of $100,000. His or her cash value increases until it reaches an amount of $22,542 at age 65. At any point the insured can take all or part of the cash value of the policy without cashing in the policy or having the death benefit reduced.

An alternative is shown as Option B. Under this option the cash value accumulates at a lower rate than under Option A, but the death benefit is in-

Table 32
Comparison of Various Options of Universal Life

Age	Annual Premium	Cash Value	Death Benefit
OPTION A—LEVEL DEATH BENEFIT			
40	$507	$ 2,236	$100,000
45	507	5,279	100,000
50	507	8,870	100,000
55	507	12,993	100,000
65	507	22,542	100,000
OPTION B—SAME PREMIUM AS OPTION A			
40	$507	$ 2,317	$102,317
45	507	5,227	105,227
50	507	8,679	108,679
55	507	12,423	112,423
65	507	19,181	119,181
OPTION B—LARGER PREMIUM THAN OPTION A			
40	$839	$ 4,301	$104,301
45	839	10,001	110,001
50	839	17,367	117,367
55	839	26,601	126,601
65	839	51,865	151,865

SOURCE: Table 5, "Universal Life—Option A vs Option B," *Life Insurance: How to Buy the Right Policy from the Right Company at the Right Price,* Lieberman, Trudy and the Editors of Consumer Report Books, Mount Vernon, NY, 1988, p. 92.

creased by the amount of the cash value. At age 65, in this option, the cash benefit is $19,181, but the death benefit is $119,181. However, should the insured borrow against the cash value, the death benefit will decline by the amount borrowed.

Universal life premiums can increase.—The premiums of universal life policies can increase unexpectedly if the company experiences unexpected increases in costs. Insurance costs must always be met by the amount of the premium. When insurance costs increase, the cash value is used to permit the premium to remain constant. However, if the cash value declines to $0, premiums can increase.

Universal life policies permit the insured to pay additional premiums in order to increase the amount of the cash value. This is shown as Option B, with larger premiums. We see that for the same basic death benefit of $100,000, the insured pays $839 in annual premiums. However, the cash value of $51,865 at age 65 is substantially higher than when the premiums are lower.

Summary

This chapter has shown the major alternative types of life insurance policies being offered. The decision on which type of insurance policy to buy should be made after the family determines how much insurance the family needs. Cost and the family's interest in investment are the principal matters for consideration. If the family is able to put aside funds for investing in a systematic way, then term policies are the best buy. However, if the family wants a forced savings vehicle, then the universal life insurance policy may be desirable. The least attractive insurance policy is likely to be a whole life policy.

The Christian family must shop carefully for insurance for its family needs. It must also look at several alternative policies and then prayerfully and carefully choose a policy that meets its needs. Remember:

IF THE INSURANCE POLICY DOES NOT MEET YOUR NEEDS, CHANGE THE POLICY, THE COMPANY, OR BOTH. DON'T CONTINUE WITH AN INSURANCE POLICY THAT DOESN'T MEET YOUR NEEDS. HOWEVER, ALWAYS HAVE SOME TYPE OF LIFE INSURANCE.

16

PREPARATION FOR RETIREMENT

For many workers retirement is best summed up by the words of the selfish rich man. He had set aside funds and goods for his retirement years, but he had neglected the poor, the disadvantaged, and those who could have benefited from some of his surplus. His selfishness nevertheless points up a major problem facing every person who works for wages or a salary and those who depend on them—what is the best time to prepare for when your wage earnings end and retirement begins?

The Christian worker who is awaiting the Lord's return may not like the idea of putting aside funds for retirement or spending a great deal of time thinking and preparing for retirement. But we do not know when our Lord will return. We do not know how long we will be retired. The prudent Christian worker will prepare for the time of retirement. If the Lord should come before retirement starts, then what has been lost? But if there is not prudent preparation for retirement, the Christian worker may find that his or her last years are years of worry and are far from "golden."

Several important issues about retirement will be considered in this chapter. The topic of retirement covers virtually all aspects of financial planning. Just as retirement is the culmination of the work life, so the topic of retirement is the culmination of financial planning.

The following are the major topics for this chapter:

- How long can you expect to be retired?
- What kind of lifestyle will you have while retired?
- How much will it cost you while you are retired?
- What are some of the health costs you will encounter?
- Where will the money come from?

- How can you develop a comprehensive plan for your retirement years?

Ages and Stages of Life

When the Christian worker or family starts to think about retirement, it is important to focus on the major stages of life.

MAJOR STAGES OF LIFE

LEARNING	EARNING	EMPTY NEST	ENJOYING
Birth	Child Rearing		Death

The learning years.—The first stage of life—the years of formal education—will last for different periods of time for different individuals and for different reasons. Half the population has 12.7 years of education, most of which begins at age 6. This suggests that by age 19, the earning years will begin for this half. For others, additional years of college extend this period until age 22. Some will continue the learning years until age 30 or later, but for the vast majority of workers the earning years begin no later than age 25. However, virtually all studies show that on average the longer a worker is in school, the more he or she will earn once the work life commences.

The earning years.—For the most part, unless you are on charity, all the money you will have during retirement will result from the earnings that you have had during your career. Because of this stark reality, the following is a good rule for thinking about retirement.

ONCE THE EARNING YEARS BEGIN, THE WORKER SHOULD START PREPARING FOR RETIREMENT.

It is very difficult for young workers, fresh from school, to think seriously about retirement. However, if young workers start thinking about retirement very early, then all future jobs will be taken with a view toward how the pension and retirement benefits will assist them to achieve their retirement goals.

The earning years are that way station in life between learning and enjoying the fruits of one's labors. For all too many workers the earning years are a drudgery. For many, work is something to be avoided or barely tolerated. But the Christian worker knows that God is the author of honest work (Gen. 3:17, 19; Ex. 20:9; Prov. 21:8). It was given to us so that our most important faculties can be developed. The rest that comes during retirement is to be the sweet reward of a life spent fulfilling God's desires for us.

During the learning years people are supported by parent(s) or guardian(s). During the earning years workers are supported by their own efforts or by the efforts of someone else. For workers in the labor market, these are the years for putting aside the funds necessary to support the retirement years. Retirement competes with raising children for the funds of the family. Since retirement seems such a long way off, usually the children win out. The all-too-unfortunate result is that there are no funds for retirement until the children are educated and independent.

For the worker who starts earning at age 25, there are about 40 working years. Not all these 40 years are spent working, since many workers have spells of unemployment and job search. But this is about all the time that a person has to prepare for retirement. The important thing to remember is that no matter how old you are or how long you have been working, you can always get started on a retirement program.

The empty nest.—Once the children are grown, the parents may spend more time on their own with such activities as travel. This is also a time when a greater amount of earnings can be set aside for retirement. The family may trade in the larger house and move to a smaller one that may cost less or require less upkeep. This is also a time to establish hobbies or activities that one will enjoy during retirement.

The length of the empty nest period will vary according to when the children are born and the number of children. In 1987 only 35 percent of all families had children under 18 (*Statistical Abstract of the United States*, Table 64). Although younger families were far more likely to have children, more than 10 percent of all families in which the head of the household was between 55 and 64 years old had children under 18 living at home.

The empty nest years generally begin when the householder is about 55 years old. This usually leaves between 5 and 10 years of the empty nest period before retirement. If the family has not set aside adequate retirement funds or an adequate pension, this is the last opportunity.

The enjoying years.—Since we do not know how long we will live, we cannot be sure how long retirement will last. Many a worker has said, like the foolish man in Luke, "Take life easy," only to have retirement cut short!

We can know something, though, about the expected length of the retirement years. Actuarial tables suggest how long males and females can expect to live under normal conditions. These expected years will vary by whether the worker is White or Black, as shown in Table 33.

Table 33
Life Expectancy at Different Ages by Race and Sex
(years)

	MALES	FEMALES	AVERAGE
	Life expectancy at age 40		
White	34.9	40.5	37.4
Black	30.3	36.6	
	Life expectancy at age 60		
White	18.2	22.6	20.4
Black	16.1	20.3	
	Life expectancy at age 65		
White	14.8	18.7	16.8
Black	13.4	17.0	

SOURCE: *Statistical Abstract of the United States* (1989) Table 109.

If a worker reaches age 60, males can expect to live about 17 more years, and females can expect to live about 21 more years. If the worker reaches age 65, on average he can expect to live for almost 14 more years, while she can expect to live for 18 more years. (How long you can expect to live is conditional on the age you are.) In 1987 there were more than 1 million individuals who were over 85 years old, and the number is rising. For those workers with a Christian lifestyle, there is reason to believe that the expected life span will be even longer.

How Much Money Will You Need for Your Retirement?

How much you will need for your retirement is one of the most difficult questions that you can ask. Most people don't have a clue. If too much is put aside for retirement, then current consumption is reduced. If current consumption is too large, then retirement income is likely to be inadequate.

THE AMOUNT OF RETIREMENT INCOME REQUIRED FOR A FAMILY IS GOING TO VARY WITH THE FAMILY'S CURRENT INCOME AND ITS DESIRED RETIREMENT LIFESTYLE.

Start with your current income.—A good place to start deciding what your retirement income should be is with your current income. If you are 40 years old, you may not have much intuition about what your future income is likely to be, much less what your retirement income should look like. That's OK. Start with your current income, make some adjustments, and then set up a retirement program that lets you live similar to the way you are living now.

Once you are retired, certain expenses will go down while others increase. For example, work related expenses—transportation to work, work clothes, and work-based taxes—will decline. On the other hand, certain expenses will go up. Chief among them will be medical expenses. Although the government provides Medicare for those over 65 years of age, there are expenses that Medicare doesn't cover. Prescription drugs may also constitute a larger percent of the family income than before retirement.

Exhibit 26
Changes in Daily Expenses During Retirement

EXPENSES LIKELY TO DECREASE	EXPENSES LIKELY TO INCREASE
Work-related expenses, such as work clothes, travel to and from work	Health related items, including medicine, drugs, and trips to the doctor's office
Social Security and other work-related taxes	Vacation-related travel
Housing costs if your house is paid for, or if you are living in a smaller residence	Household assistance, including cleaning and yard-related expenses

Your tax bill during retirement will decrease but not necessarily stop.

Most of your retirement income will not be taxed if it comes from pensions or Social Security. If, however, it comes from interest, dividends, or work, then you can expect to pay taxes. The amount of taxes you will pay will depend on how much your total income is and the sources of that income. Of course, consumption taxes—like sales taxes—will continue.

Because it is not possible to determine just what the increases and decreases are likely to be, the following guideline is often used. (It must be remembered that this is true only if there are no taxes paid during retirement and if there are no other major expenses.)

As a general rule, during retirement you will need 70 percent of your after-tax, earnings-years income.

What this means for monthly income is shown in Table 35. If you were retiring in 1993 and had a monthly income of $1,250 before taxes and $940 after taxes, you would need about $660 each month while you are retired to enjoy a lifestyle comparable to what you are enjoying now. If your monthly income is $6,000 in 1993, you would need $3,150 each month that you are retired. To figure out approximately how much you will actually need, take a look at your monthly take-home pay (subtract federal taxes, Social Security taxes, and state and local taxes from your gross earnings) and multiply it by 0.70. That is the amount you will need.

Retirement and inflation.—But hold on a minute! This is what you will need during the first month of your retirement *if* you retire in *1994*. Each month after you retire, the cost of living will be going up. Each year it will cost you, on average, 4.5 percent more for all the things you buy—*if* present inflation rates continue. If inflation should get worse, you will need even more. If you retire five, 10, or 20 years from now, the amount that you will need will be larger still.

How much you will need will depend on the composition of your family, your lifestyle, where you will live, and the level of inflation between now and the time that you actually retire. No one knows what these things will be. But we can say something about inflation and the role it will play in the quality of your retirement.

What if you are not retiring this year?—The amounts shown previously are for those who are retiring this year. To determine how much you will need in actual dollars when you get ready to retire, multiply the amount given earlier by the age factor in Exhibit 27.

Table 34
Monthly Needs During Your Retirement Years

Average Current Gross Income	Average Current Take Home Income	Amount of Retirement Income Needed
$ 1,000	$ 750	$ 600
1,500	1,125	900
2,000	1,500	1,200
2,500	1,875	1,500
3,000	2,250	1,800
3,500	2,625	2,100
4,000	2,760	2,208
4,500	2,745	2,196
5,000	3,050	2,440
5,500	3,493	2,794
6,000	3,810	3,048
6,500	4,128	3,302
7,000	4,445	3,556
7,500	4,763	3,810
8,000	5,080	4,064
8,500	5,398	4,318
9,000	5,715	4,572
9,500	6,033	4,826
10,000	6,350	5,080

NOTE: Assumes Social Security taxes of 7.5%, income taxes of 14% and 28% at higher incomes, and state and local taxes at 3.5%.

Exhibit 27
Factors to Determine Future Retirement Income

If your age is	Use this as a multiplier	If your age is	Use this as a multiplier
35	4.32	50	2.08
36	4.12	51	1.98
37	3.92	52	1.89
38	3.73	53	1.80
39	3.56	54	1.71
40	3.39	55	1.63
41	3.23	56	1.55
42	3.07	57	1.48
43	2.93	58	1.41
44	2.79	59	1.34
45	2.65	60	1.28
46	2.53	61	1.21
47	2.41	62	1.15
48	2.29	63	1.10
49	2.18	64	1.05

For example, suppose you are 45 years old and your current income is $5,000 a month, with take-home pay of $3,050. If you retire at age 65 and follow the suggested retirement income amount, you will need $2,440 of current, nontaxed income each month. Look up the factor for a person 45 years old—it is 2.65. Multiply 2.65 times $2,440 to get the amount $5,466 a month. This is how much 45-year-olds who earn $5,000 now will need each month upon retirement. This is only an approximation, based on an inflation rate of 5 percent. If inflation is higher, you will need more.

Inflation is likely to continue after you retire.—Wait, there's more. The needs shown in Table 34 are the needs for the *first year* that you retire. If you live your expected 14 to 18 years after retirement, inflation will continue to stalk you. By the time today's 45-year-olds have reached age 75, there will be 10 years of additional inflation to cope with. And we know what inflation can do!

What is the Christian family to do? First, we need to know something about where the funds will come from. Next, we need to know something about how those funds will be impacted by inflation.

Where Will the Retirement Funds Come From?

The major sources of retirement funds for individuals over 65 are:

- Social Security
- employment-generated pensions/annuities
- savings and investments
- employment
- supplemental security income (welfare)

What is Social Security?—Social Security is a federal program that pays retirement income to U.S. workers who have accumulated 40 quarters or more of work. Social Security is inflation-indexed so that the benefit amounts increase by the amount of inflation (if inflation is greater than 3 percent).

Social Security is provided for the wage earner, his or her surviving spouse, and dependent children who are age 18 or under. The amount of the Social Security payment is based on the worker's highest three-year level of income. There is a minimum and a maximum Social Security payment, with the maximum approximating $2,267 a month for a worker and spouse in 1993.

Will Social Security alone be enough?—Social Security alone will generally *not be enough* to continue the family in a lifestyle comparable to that which it had during the employment years. To attain the maximum Social Security payment, the family in 1993 must have had an indexed income equivalent to at least $55,500, or about $5,000 a month. According to Table 34, the income needed at retirement to replace this level of wage income is at least $2,440. This means that under the best of conditions, the family that has the maximum Social Security will cover these costs.

A CHRISTIAN FAMILY WHOSE ONLY SOURCE OF INCOME IS SOCIAL SECURITY MAY NOT BE IN POVERTY, BUT IT MAY NOT BE ABLE TO AFFORD MANY OF THE THINGS THAT MAKE RETIREMENT LIFE INTERESTING.

How do you get Social Security?—

- You should find out immediately how much money you would likely receive when you are ready to retire.

- You should find out how many quarters of earnings you now have and your eligibility for benefits.

All these things—and more—you can get from your local Social Security office. The number for the nearest Social Security office or of an 800 number to call to get information is found in the telephone book.

What about employment-based pensions?—There are several ways that you can have a pension from employment-based activities: (1) the employer makes contributions toward your pension; (2) you make contributions, and they are matched or supplemented by the employer; or (3) you set up an independent 401(k) plan and make contributions to your pension.

As is true of Social Security, you should get from your employer information about the amount of any pension funds that the employer is setting aside for you.

TO AS LARGE AN EXTENT AS POSSIBLE, TAKE ADVANTAGE OF ANY MATCHING FUNDS THAT AN EMPLOYER MAY SET ASIDE FOR YOU. IN THE ABSENCE OF EMPLOYER CONTRIBUTIONS, SET UP YOUR OWN PROGRAM.

What is a 401(k) plan?—Under federal law you are allowed to establish a tax-deferred pension plan for yourself in which you may set aside up to 10 percent of your income toward retirement. Funds set aside are subtracted from your gross income before taxes. Taxes are not taken out until you start receiving the funds at retirement. If you wish to set up a 401(k) program, consult the retirement office of your employer or a specialist in pension plans.

How long will you be able to work?—Employment is not a very good option for supporting your retirement. However, if you have not prepared carefully, it may be an unfortunate last resort. But if you live long enough, the chances are that you will not be able to continue to work. Working during retirement is not desirable and may not be feasible for some. A tragedy of too many workers is to work without having earned a rest.

Do you qualify for welfare?—Supplemental security income is available to persons over 65 who have no other forms of income. It is a welfare payment to the elderly that is far less generous than Social Security payments. If you do not plan for your retirement, you may qualify for welfare.

Putting It All Together

The ideal pension program is one in which *one third* comes from Social Security, *one third* comes from pensions, and *one third* comes from accumulated savings. Unlike Social Security, few pension plans have cost-of-living adjustments (COLAs). As a result, the family must choose how it will receive its pension funds and how it will invest its accumulated savings to permit it to have a financial worry-free retirement.

What Is an Annuity?

An annuity is a series of equal payments made at fixed intervals. For retired persons it is a scheduled payment throughout the life of the individual or for a preset period of time. If an annuity is set for the life of the individual, it will be less than if is set for a preset period of time. Most whole life insurance plans and many pension plans pay out their benefits in the form of an annuity.

The amount of benefits received by the retiree will depend on the size of the accumulated benefits, the payout schedule, and the terms of the payout. An annuity can be for the remaining life of the individual or for a fixed period of time.

For a given amount of accumulated funds, if an annuity is to have guaranteed payout for the rest of the retiree's life, it will pay less per year than the same size annuity that provides guaranteed benefits for a fixed number of years. If the retiree selects the larger amount of money each year, then this introduces a particular problem associated with annuities:

A MAJOR PROBLEM FOR RETIREES IS THAT THEY SOMETIMES OUTLIVE THEIR MONEY!

What Is a Perpetuity?

The payout from an insurance or pension plan can be made in the form of a perpetuity.

A perpetuity is a never-ending payment that is a fixed percent of a principal amount. The payment of a perpetuity is defined as:

PAYMENT = INTEREST X PRINCIPAL

When a payout is in the form of a perpetuity, then it is guaranteed to last for the life of the retired individual, and once that individual is deceased the principal is left intact! In other words, a retiree can set up a $200,000 estate that pays 10 percent interest, receive $20,000 from that estate for as long as he or she lives, and the estate still have $200,000 left once the retiree dies. That $200,000 can then be used by an heir for as long as the heir lives—still receiving $20,000 per year—and this can continue in perpetuity.

In a perpetuity the retiree lives on the interest derived from the principal. The principal is never touched. However, from our discussion on inflation, it is clear that the purchasing power is continually being eroded. Thus, although the principal remains the same, it buys less and less. If the retiree lives for 15 years on the principal, the payment will be worth only a fraction of its value at the beginning of the period.

Comparing Annuities and Perpetuities

Annuities and perpetuities each have particular advantages and disadvantages for the retiree. For a given amount of cash, an annuity provides a higher annual income, but will eventually run out. A perpetuity, on the other hand, will never run out, but will provide smaller annual payments. In addition, the perpetuity will retain the principal to be given to heirs or left for a bequest.

An annuity can be set up so that it is adjusted for inflation or not adjusted. When an annuity is adjusted for inflation, the family will maintain the same standard of living throughout the life of the annuity.

SOCIAL SECURITY OPERATES LIKE A LIFETIME ANNUITY THAT IS ANNUALLY ADJUSTED FOR THE COST OF LIVING.

How Much Cash Will You Need?

The retired family will need a large amount of money to finance their retirement. Various amounts are shown in Table 35.

Here's an example of how to interpret Table 35. Let us suppose the family wishes to have $2,000 per month during its retirement.

Plan 1. Choose a perpetuity.

If it chooses a perpetuity, then it will have to purchase $240,000 in bonds paying 10 percent per year. Each spouse and survivor will have

$2,000 per month, and there will still be $240,000 in bonds to will to heirs or to bequest. However, the purchasing power of the income will steadily erode. In 10 years that $2,000 will purchase only the equivalent of $1,300; in 15 years, only about $1,000.

Table 35
Amount of Cash Needed to Purchase Perpetuity or Annuity

		ANNUITIES					
		10 Years		15 Years		20 Years	
Monthly Income	Perpetuities	Not Adjusted	Adjusted	Not Adjusted	Adjusted	Not Adjusted	Adjusted
$ 600	$ 72,000	$ 45,403	$ 58,923	$ 55,834	$ 79,568	$ 62,175	$ 95,928
800	96,000	60,537	77,692	74,446	105,217	82,900	127,031
1,000	120,000	75,671	97,115	93,057	131,522	103,625	158,789
1,200	144,000	90,805	116,538	111,669	157,826	124,350	190,546
1,500	180,000	113,507	145,672	139,586	197,283	155,437	238,183
2,000	240,000	151,342	194,229	186,115	263,044	207,249	317,577
2,500	300,000	189,178	242,787	232,644	328,805	259,062	396,972
3,000	360,000	227,013	291,344	279,172	394,566	310,874	476,366
3,500	420,000	264,849	339,901	325,701	460,327	362,686	555,760
4,000	480,000	302,685	388,458	372,230	526,087	414,498	635,154
5,000	600,000	378,356	485,573	465,287	657,609	518,123	793,943

SOURCE: Calculations by the author. "Adjusted" means that the amount is adjusted for a 5% inflation rate per year. "Unadjusted" means that the initial amount of funds will diminish at the same 5% inflation rate. By their very nature, perpetuities are not adjusted for inflation.

Plan 2. Choose an annuity.

If the family decides to purchase an annuity, it must first decide the number of years for the annuity, then whether or not it wants to have its funds adjusted for inflation. A 10-year annuity that is not adjusted for inflation will cost $151,342. A 15-year unadjusted annuity will cost $186,115; for 20 years it will cost $207,249. Like the perpetuity, such an annuity will steadily erode in value. Should one or both members of the family outlive the annuity period, there will be no more money from this source!

If the family decides to purchase an inflation-adjusted annuity, the cost will rise dramatically. For a 10-year annuity, it will cost $194,229; for a 15-year annuity the cost goes up to $263,044; and for a 20-year annuity the cost would be a whopping $317,577. The family will continue to maintain a constant living standard, but like any annuity, at the end of the annuity period the money will be gone.

Plan 3. An annuity that looks like a perpetuity.

The longer the period of an unadjusted annuity, the more it returns the same value of a perpetuity. For example, a 20-year annuity that returns $2,000 per month costs $207,249. But with that same amount of funds, the family can purchase 10 percent bonds that will pay $1,727 per month for as long as either partner lives and still have the $207,249 to leave as a bequest.

The information in Table 35 shows clearly that the family has many choices and combinations for financing its retirement. This is true if the source of funds is from a pension, the cashing out of an insurance plan, or the results of savings.

The family that has limited retirement funds has to decide what its priorities are. It has to decide the extent that it wishes to trade off a constant standard of living against the assurance that there will always be some funds available. It also has to decide whether it wants to leave a bequest for heirs or institutions.

Liquidating bonds as an option.—One popular option for dealing with the dilemma of whether to choose a perpetuity or an annuity is to choose a series of liquidating bonds. Under this option the retiree buys a series of bonds that expire over a period ranging from one to 25 years. The retiree draws down the principal and interest of the bonds as they mature. This permits the retiree to mature the bonds as needed for living expenses or to reinvest them for future income or bequests. It is highly recommended that in the execution of such a plan, the retiree use a highly reputable investment trustee.

Where is the money going to come from?—The amount of funds suggested for retirement, even in 1992 dollars, is quite large. The average family is not likely to accumulate the hundreds of thousands of dollars necessary to support a comfortable retirement without careful planning. The most popular sources of retirement funds are Social Security, employment-provided pensions, self-financed IRA and 401(k) plans, life insurance payouts, and other savings or investments. These plans can be enhanced with prudent payout schedules.

At What Age Should You Retire?

There is a longstanding tradition of retiring at age 65. Yet there is nothing magical about that age. Indeed, many workers are retiring earlier or later. Nowadays the choice is up to the worker. More and more workers are retiring at any point between the ages of 60 and 70. The Age Discrimination Act discourages mandatory retirement ages for workers.

THE LAWS OF THE LAND PERMIT YOU TO RETIRE WHENEVER YOU WANT UNDER MOST CIRCUMSTANCES. YOU DON'T HAVE TO RETIRE AT A SET AGE!

There are three very real considerations that you must take into account when you start thinking about retiring: (1) your physical, mental, and emotional ability to work; (2) your ability to finance retirement; and (3) the cost to you of retiring early.

Each worker differs in his or her ability to continue to perform productively as he or she ages. For some workers, abilities slow dramatically after age 60; others, however, are at their mental peaks. Remember, many presidents of the United States, corporate executives, professors, members of Congress, and other workers have served well long into their 60s.

The worker should weigh carefully whether or not financing plans are in place to permit retirement at a given age. A financial assessment such as illustrated in this book will tell whether the worker can afford to retire early—or even at all!

Social Security payments and most pension plans provide smaller pensions if the worker retires early. As noted earlier, Social Security reduces the worker's payments by 7 percent for each year that the worker retires before 65 up to a 20 percent reduction in benefits. Even then, benefits can start only at age 62.

THE MAJOR COST OF RETIRING EARLY IS THAT THE BENEFIT BASE IS REDUCED. SUBSEQUENT COST-OF-LIVING ADJUSTMENTS ARE SMALLER.

For some workers it is worth it to begin early the greater leisure activities associated with retirement. Each worker will have to decide with his or her family what is best.

Conclusion

Plan wisely for your retirement. In this life it is the only retirement you will have. Start planning now.

17

PLANNING YOUR ESTATE

"This is what the Lord says: Put your house in order, because you are going to die; you will not recover" (Isa. 38:1). Hezekiah was sick, and Isaiah told him that he would die. The king was directed by the Lord to make plans for the disposal of his estate. Christians seldom get so direct an order to plan for their estate!

Even though there may not be a direct command, the message is the same: Until the Lord returns, each one of us will die. Each one of us will need to make plans for our estate.

What Is an Estate?

From this definition it is clear that an estate can exist while the person is alive or is created as an object that has legal standing after the person is deceased.

AN ESTATE IS ANY RIGHT, TITLE, OR OTHER INTEREST IN REAL OR PERSONAL PROPERTY. IT IS ALSO THE SUM OF ALL ASSETS OWNED BY AN INDIVIDUAL AT THE TIME OF HIS OR HER DEATH MINUS ANY LIABILITIES.

An estate, under the law, can be any size as long as it contains real or personal property. When the estate is small, consisting largely of personal items, its disposition is often carried out informally by the survivors. However, when the estate becomes sizable and includes cash or things easily converted into cash, there are rules on how the assets in the estate are to be distributed.

What Is Estate Planning?

Estate planning involves making plans for:

- the creation of a viable estate
- the care of minor children
- the final disposition of one's physical remains
- the settlement of one's liabilities
- the distribution of one's assets
- an administrator for the estate
- minimizing tax impacts on estates

Estate planning can be summarized by the method used to develop an estate plan and when and how the plan is executed.

Exhibit 28

Method to Develop an Estate Plan	When the Plan Is Executed and Its Major Features
A Living Trust	Executed during the life of the trustor. Usually revocable, it transfers assets to a trustee who then administers the estate on behalf of the trustor. A lawyer is usually required to establish a trust. There are no special tax advantages to a living trust. However, it avoids probate and thus saves the estate money. The trust, however, may permit the individual to be relieved of some of the requirements of financial management.
A Will	Established by the testator and becomes effective upon death of the testator. Usually the most versatile instrument for accomplishing the testator's wishes. The will expresses the desires of the maker for the disposal of his or her assets and the care of dependent children after his or her death. A lawyer is usually required to set up a will.
Intestate	No established will or trust; when the person dies intestate the state in which he or she lived will use the laws of that state to determine what happens to the estate, including what happens to dependent children. To die intestate is to be dependent on the state.

Creation of a Viable Estate

A viable estate is one that provides for the care and support of individuals dependent on the estatemaker and one that accomplishes the wishes of the estatemaker. An estate can be small or large. No one knows when he or she will die. Thus, no one knows what the size of the estate will be at the time of death.

The following steps are essential in the creation of a viable estate:

- establishment of a set of goals.
- determination of the tax consequences of the estate plan.
- establishment of a timetable to accomplish goals.
- review of the estate plan to adjust for changing circumstances.

The Christian family should always be aware that too much energy and effort devoted to preparing an estate may lessen the interest in things eternal. An estate plan should be developed, but it should not be the focus of the Christian's life.

The chief vehicle for the accomplishment of an estate plan is the written will. When you have a will, there is a way to accomplish your objectives according to your wishes. When you do not have a will, the objectives will be accomplished by the laws of the state. The state's will is not likely to be yours.

But estate planning is not some stuffy activity that makes plans only for the individual's death. Estate planning—if carried out to its highest and best—means that the Christian family can witness how God's blessings can go to further His work, how the children in the family can be made more productive, and how a living legacy can be created while the individual and spouse are alive.

Care for minor children.—One of the greatest legacies given to us by a loving God is the ability to reproduce children after our own kind and to raise them in the care and admonition of the Lord (Eph. 6:4; Prov. 22:6). An estate plan, therefore, should include provisions for any minor children.

If children are not provided for in an estate plan (for example, in the event of a sudden death), the state may assign the children to individuals who do not share the Christian beliefs of the parents. A guardian selected by the state need not raise the children in the way that you would have had you lived.

Once a decision is made, the family should talk with the prospective guardian. The family's wishes regarding how they want the children raised as it relates to church attendance, church schools, college, and other such issues should be discussed. If the prospective guardian agrees to your wishes, he or she should be listed in the will as guardian of the minor children in the event of the death of both parents. Financial provisions should be made for the care of such children.

IN DEVELOPING AN ESTATE PLAN, DISCUSS WITH THE FAMILY MEMBERS WHO SHOULD CARE FOR MINOR CHILDREN IN THE EVENT OF THE PREMATURE DEATH OF THE PARENTS. CHILDREN'S VIEWS SHOULD BE CONSIDERED IN THIS DECISION.

Final disposition of physical remains.—Few things are as distasteful as thinking about one's funeral. Yet in the absence of an estate plan that expresses your wishes, these necessary arrangements can cause undue hardship on your survivors during their moment of grief. While none of us knows the time or manner of our death, there are some things that we should give thought to.

- Anatomical gifts. There is a continuing need for organ donors. You may actually carry a donor card that specifies your intent to permit your organs to be donated to needy recipients in the event of your death. Such a decision can be made by you or your survivors. Your wishes in this matter should be stated, although they may not be followed.
- Burial Plots. Many families purchase burial plots with the intention that the husband, wife, and possibly other family members will be interred in a common area. There are several advantages and disadvantages to owning these plots.

Advantages:

- Having a plot simplifies a critical decision that has to be made during a very stressful time.
- There may be some cost savings involved with choosing a plot, especially if land prices are rising faster than the rate of inflation.

Disadvantages:

- Couples break up and sometimes remarry. When this happens, the children may want the parents buried in the same plot. However, the last spouse has the final say. It can get ugly.
- Families move.

Many times a Christian wishes to be remembered as he or she has lived—a person of simple style who would want a funeral that does not impose a financial burden on survivors. Funeral services can cost many thousands of dollars and reduce critical funds needed by survivors in the days following death. An estate plan can express your wishes, even though it need not be followed to the letter.

SURVIVORS ARE NOT BOUND BY THE TERMS OF A WILL IN THE DISPOSITION OF YOUR FINAL REMAINS. HOWEVER, YOUR WISHES SHOULD BE MADE KNOWN. BURYING YOU SHOULD NOT ALSO BURY THE FAMILY FINANCIALLY.

Discussion should also be made regarding the nature of the service and which persons should participate. For the Christian, such issues as cremation should be discussed. Many Christians do not regard cremation as an acceptable means of disposal of their final physical remains. These issues should be carefully considered and discussed.

Conclusion

There are numerous ways to develop an estate plan for you and your family. Because it is such an important event and involves legal as well as financial considerations, you are urged to consult legal assistance in the preparation of an estate plan. The family should enter into such a plan only after prayerfully and carefully considering all that will be required to establish an estate.

18

Here's the Conclusion of the Whole Matter

In *Making Ends Meet* we have looked at many complex subjects that involve financial matters for the Christian family. We have developed the central theme that ultimately the Christian family is a steward of God's goodness to us. In the matter of our finances we have the stirring words: "But if any provide not for his own, and specially for those of his own house, he hath denied the faith, and is worse than an infidel" (1 Tim. 5:8).

We have also developed a systematic way of looking at finances from the perspective of the time value of money. While we are admonished to be faithful stewards, life in late twentieth-century United States embodies many choices and much to know and do.

As a result, our task of providing adequately for our families and ourselves is a daunting one. For many first-time readers of a comprehensive book on finances there are the inevitable questions of Where should I begin? and What should I get out of so much material? Let me help you.

Read this book to become familiar with the general landscape of financial management as a central focus of how the Christian family will be faithful. Recognize that many of these concepts you are already putting into practice. Every family has a budget. It is either an explicit budget carefully and prayerfully developed or it is a budget that arises from the set of choices that we make.

Now that you know that these concepts are mostly a formal way of looking at many things you have already thought about, there is a systematic way to use the material you have just covered.

First, it is important not to be overwhelmed by the sheer volume of the material. Take things on a topical basis, for example. You should read chapter 2 to understand how a modern economy works and how your finances can be brought under control in a world that seems sometimes to spin out of control.

Second, remember that *Making Ends Meet* is a source book for helping you in your quest for financial freedom. As such, it is not a book to be read as one would a good story book. It is a book for referring back to when your particular circumstance dictates it. For instance, when you are thinking about buying a house, you may want to focus on the part of the book that discusses the topic. You can then master those concepts and seek additional guidance from other sources and professional advisers.

YOU DON'T HAVE TO DO EVERYTHING IN *MAKING ENDS MEET* IN ORDER TO BE SUCCESSFUL IN YOUR QUEST FOR FINANCIAL FREEDOM.

You can achieve some of the goals set forth in this book just by moving in the right direction as you understand it for your family's needs. Practice a few things, such as setting up a formal budget and seeing whether or not you can stick to it. Start a special savings account for future investing in the stock market (where the returns are much greater, on average). Learn more about creative financing for real estate.

Will *Making Ends Meet* help you achieve a better financial condition if you follow some of the ideas set forth? Only if those goals are in harmony with God's will and your understanding of your family's needs. Test out *Making Ends Meet* for one year. You will probably be very pleasantly surprised at how much better your financial picture becomes.

List of Tables

LIST OF EXHIBITS

List of Figures